G000165634

Ruth Fogg

Speaker   Therapist
Educator   Author

Published by The Visualisation Press Melville House, 2 The Glade, Staines Middlesex. TW18 1EW

ISBN: 978-1-907385-23-0   First published 2021

INTRODUCTION

As I finished "Stress N' Stuff – Tackling Tough Times" the new school year began, followed by universities resuming their studies after a longer break than usual due to the pandemic. The picture began to emerge how students were struggling and how different this academic year is in comparison to any before.

The traditional route of mock exams, applications, provisional offers, exams, results, acceptance or clearing, came unstuck. Chaos and confusion replaced normality and anxiety replaced anticipation and excitement.

It's been a long time since I was a student, but I can clearly recall leaving leafy Surrey to train to become a teacher in Bradford, West Yorkshire. It was like being in a foreign country and it took months to understand the broad Yorkshire accent! I was very homesick too and would ring home sobbing, but I stuck it out until Christmas before I went home. Strangely, it all felt better when I got back, and I thoroughly enjoyed the next three years.

The focus of this book is for young adults 18 +, who have left home to embark on University or College Life. You have already been cheated of Freshers Week and many other activities associated with the first term as well as lectures where you meet others and make friends. Online is just not the same! It will of course, be relevant to students post pandemic. Student stress is sadly here to stay, now more than ever.

The purpose of this book is to explore the WHAT, WHY, WHEN, WHO, WHERE of stress and mental health and then look at the HOW.

Feel free to dip in and out but it is important to understand HOW your mind works and WHERE your stress is coming from as well as WHY and WHAT you can do about it.

ACKNOWLEDGMENTS

Thanks as ever to my husband Nigel for his patience and endless cups of tea. Also to my son Duncan and nieces Rachel and Amy (two graduates and one pending!) for their moral support and feedback.

I would also like to acknowledge the struggle that so many students are experiencing and hope that some sense of normality returns soon so you can get on with your lives.

Ruth Fogg   January 2021

CONTENTS

1

STUDENT

STUFF

"Research that NUS published earlier this month found that student mental health has worsened over the course of the pandemic with isolation and low self-esteem increasingly common. Coronavirus has placed additional stresses on students; 82% are worried about the health of their family members, and 56% have told us they are worried about contracting the virus on campus and 3 in 4 students are worried about how they will pay their rent. The inability of government to get a grip of the situation means this is only worsening; students face growing uncertainty over access to education and their finances, and those that are locked down are going without food and basic amenities. Without immediate action we risk failing a generation. Students deserve better."

NUS President Larissa Kennedy. September 2020

Student stress in 2020 reached new heights, having to cope with situations that no-one could ever have imagined. There have been numerous surveys carried out to ascertain the levels of student stress over the years but never before like this.

Moving away from home and starting a new life at university is a stressful time for everyone, with new environments, new accommodation, and new relationships as well as new subjects. The anticipation of going to university, the excitement, hopes and dreams have been shattered by Covid-19.

Save the Student surveyed 2,076 students at the start of the academic year and 94% were affected by the virus with 66% stating that their mental health was their main concern. This was followed by a fear of passing Covid-19 onto others and loneliness.

www.savethestudent.org/money/surveys/covid-19-student-survey-follow-up.html#issues

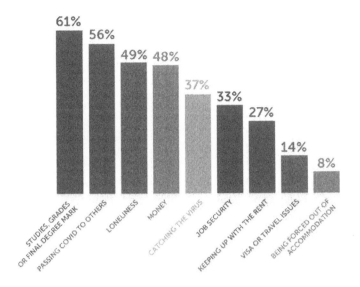

Each year the Nat West bank carries out surveys as part of a "Student Living Index". The 2020 study was influenced by the pandemic and shows that :
* Only 29% of students felt supported by their university.
* 1 in 4 believe their studies have been negatively impacted
* Only 1 in10 think they are getting value for money
* Only 33% have been offered a rent break by their landlord
* Only 27% feel they have been offered adequate mental healthcare

These findings are on top of the "normal" causes of student stress:

Curriculum
Between exams, coursework and classes, students often find themselves overloaded and exhausted.

Finances

The huge £20,000+ debts students are asked to take on today to attend university are a common cause of stress for young people.

Data overload

Gen Z are faced with the internet, smartphones, social media, and 24/7 news cycles every day which can feel like there is no escape from constant connectivity.

Post-graduation plans

Choosing the right path to take after graduation has always been a worry for students, but in the current climate and with the economy buffeted by a global pandemic and Brexit makes planning for the future harder than ever.

See the full report:
www.personal.natwest.com/personal/life-moments/
students-and-graduates/student-living-
index.html#impact-of-covid-19

In March and September 2020, the NUS carried out two surveys to assess the impact of Coronavirus on students.
www.nusconnect.org.uk/resources/covid-19-and-
students-survey-report-phase-2-public-version

It would be fair to say that things have changed significantly since this academic year began with the second surge, mass testing and travel arrangements for Christmas. 2021 will undoubtedly bring more challenges which will cast a shadow on student life.

"Students at a number of universities are unhappy with the level of mental health support they have received, with complaints about services that are hard to access, with long waiting lists or limited to 15-minute time slots. "
The Guardian November 2020

An enterprising student at Bath has set up a Facebook Page for students to share their stories **www.facebook.com/studentcovidcrisis**

So how is all this affecting you? Some universities are responding better than others and for many people, regardless of age or circumstance, this virus feels unreal – until it affects us directly. If you are kept informed and up to date on what is happening, you are more likely to feel included and valued.

There is nothing worse than seeing what is going on at your uni on national television when you had no idea of what was happening!
Keep up to date with **www.studentspace.org.uk** which is a part of **www.studentminds.org.uk**

Are you aware of the University Mental Health Charter? Check on Student Minds to see if your university has signed up to it.
Counselling services are stretched to the limit so knowing how to understand and manage your own mental health is crucial. Read on…

2

STRESS STUFF

"God will never give you anything you can't handle, so don't stress".
Kelly Clarkson

The phrase mental health has become such a familiar term to all of us in recent years with media, charities and health organisations seeking recognition for the enormity of the problem.

What does the term mental health mean to you? How do we decide who is mentally healthy and who is not?
The statistics for people suffering from mental health disorders are scary, and the Mental Health Foundation states that one in four of us experience a mental health problem each year. Fortunately, most of these situations are mild and mainly caused by anxiety and **stress.**

At the other end of the scale, however, there are serious mental health illnesses and conditions. The MIND website **www.mind.org.uk** and The Mental health Foundation **www.mentalhealth.org.uk** have detailed lists with clear explanations.

Stress levels during the pandemic inevitably increased with constant worry, fear, confusion, and distress affecting our mental health and wellbeing.
Stress had already become an everyday word as well as an everyday reality in our busy lives. It is invisible, often misunderstood, and seems to creep up on us unawares, until suddenly we can't cope anymore. It affects us all in one way or another depending on circumstances.

Before we explore stress more fully, lets look at all the changes that you have been through or are still going through as you adapt to student life. So much change in such a short time, so many different things to cope with all at once. Bombarded with information, trying to find your niche, managing a budget, living on your own, coping with homesickness, building relationships, absorbing new subjects - it's a different world.

What we tend to forget is that change is a process, and it happens, by degree, each and every day. Look how your body has changed since you were a child, think how strange and it felt on your first day at secondary school. We make changes and adapt to circumstances without realising.

Some changes in life are welcome and some are resisted. If the change is through choice, then it is much easier to adapt than when change is forced upon us as it has been with the pandemic. Enforced change causes misery, confusion and resentment as well as stress because we feel no ownership of the process..

Have a look at the steps below which are recognised as the "change process" (*O'Connor 1998 adapted from Kubler-Ross 1969*). Can you identify with them?

1. Stability - This precedes the actual change. (pre pandemic)

2. Immobilisation - A sense of disbelief, unreality and often shock. This can vary from temporary confusion to complete disorientation. (March 2020 onwards)

3. Denial - There is an inability to relate to what is happening around us. (The increasing death rate is difficult to comprehend and feels unreal)

4. Anger - (*Not what you signed up for?*) frustration and hurt can push people away.

5. Bargaining - this is the beginning of acceptance whilst considering and exploring the possible positive outcomes of the new situation. *(Trying to make it work)*

6. Depression - This is a normal response to change when it is perceived as negative.
There may be a sense of failure, victimisation, loss as well as low energy and disengagement. Once we get through this stage, we are moving towards acceptance.

7. Testing - We start to move forward and create new objectives/ goals which brings back a sense of control.

8. Acceptance - We now respond to the change realistically, we may not like it but we accept it.

Change is stressful but once the dust has settled and things become more familiar, this stress goes away. Of course, there are numerous other causes of stress. Rushing in the morning for lectures, (in normal times) poor relationships, forgetting where you left things, worrying about money, cancelled buses or trains, traffic hold-ups, being late for everything, arguments with friends, family, misunderstandings, unfair criticism, exam pressure, work demands, high expectations, not feeling good enough, not fitting in, lack of appreciation, too much to do, not enough time... the list goes on and on, whatever age we are.

"God, grant me the serenity to accept the things I cannot change, courage to change the things I can, and wisdom to know the difference".
Reinhold Niebuhr

Because stress has become an everyday part of our lives, many of us see and accept it as being normal and don't realise that it can be managed and, in many cases, eliminated!

What is stressful for one person may be perfectly acceptable to another; indeed, some people seem to thrive on living under pressure or stress and others seem to go to pieces over the slightest little thing. Stress is not only triggered by events and experiences, but also how we react to these situations. If we could identify the triggers and where they come from – we would be halfway there!

The situations that make us feel stressed gradually build up and eventually become too much to cope with, causing anxiety, panic attacks, headaches, depression and other stress-related behaviours and illnesses.

Not all stress is bad. We need a certain amount of it to get us going, to get the best out of us. It is a degree of stress that gets us up on a cold winter's morning when the alarm goes off, that motivates us to get to places on time, and without stress we can become apathetic, lethargic and lazy.

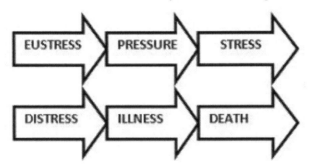

Stress is by degree, *Eustress* is the positive which can be described as that buzz you feel when something exciting happens or is about to happen, like a child waking on Christmas morning. *Distress, Illness, Burnout and Death are* of course, the negative manifestations if stress is not dealt with. There is also Post Traumatic Stress, which, as its name suggests, can occur because of a past traumatic experience or event.

You might feel yourself to be under constant pressure and unable to cope with the demands of today's fast and hectic lifestyle. Alternatively. You may love it!

Spending thirty weeks of the year (on average) at university can be stressful, having to meet the demands of lectures, tutorials and workload as well as taking care of yourself, (maybe for the first time). You may be living or working with people you do not particularly like. Added to that is budgeting, feeding yourself, doing laundry and keeping in touch with friends and family back at home.

It seems strange that when we have so many time-saving, labour-saving devices, computers, washing machines, microwaves, tumble dryers, dishwashers, fast cars, to name but a few, many of us still find it difficult to enjoy quality time doing what we really want to do. How much time have we gained from these inventions? When we do have spare time, how many of us feel guilty when we are inactive or doing something for ourselves?

Technology and Social Media are time thieves – how often do you switch off your mobile phone or tablet?! It's stressful when it's on and even more so when it's off, wondering who may have been trying to contact you. Are you a victim of FOMO (fear of missing out)?

Many people today are suffering from information overload – too much for the brain to cope with. We wake up feeling overwhelmed and go to bed feeling the same.

Dr. Hans Seyle (1907 -1982) was the "father" of stress who identified the General Adaptation Syndrome theory in 1936 when he realised that most illnesses were linked to stressful experiences or circumstances. The three stages were Alarm, Resistance and Exhaustion.

There are numerous stress tests online, the most famous of which are Holmes and Rae 1967 and Coopers Life Stress Inventory 1988. Have a look at the Stressworx Stress profile.

How stressed are you?

Have a look at the table below and answer as honestly as you can

5 = All the time 4 = Often 3 = Sometimes
2 = Rarely 1 = Never

Do you....	5	4	3	2	1
Feel upset and moody?					
Feel cheated by the virus?					
Feel confused and/ or angry?					
Resent the debt you will have?					
Get migraines/headaches?					
Find it hard to concentrate?					
Sleep badly?					
Avoid your friends? Get irritated easily?					
Feel anxious?					
Take time off lectures?					
Feel fed up?					
Feel isolated?					
Think that things are all your fault?					
Feel overwhelmed?					
Feel tired all the time?					
Eating or drinking too much?					
Feel physically sick and wound up?					
Lose your appetite?					
Snap at those close to you?					
Feel that life is pointless?					

Feel that you just can't cope?				
Get angry easily?				
Feel worthless?				
Feel nervous?				
Keep problems to yourself?				
Argue with friend or family?				
Feel scared of your thoughts?				
Take drugs to escape reality?				
Cry a lot?				
Feel you need anti-depressants?				
Feel suicidal?				
Self-harm?				
Get muscle aches and pains?				
Feel sad for no reason?				
Have a nervous stomach?				
Get rashes?				
Get palpitations?				
Feel panicky?				
Have nightmares/bad dreams?				
Worry about failure?				
Other symptoms?				

If most of your ticks are in the first three columns, then you are probably experiencing an unhealthy level of stress in your life and its time to take some action!

Kanner et al 1981 identified "Daily Hassles" as a more likely predictor of stress related problems as opposed to major events. The Transactional Model of Stress (Lazarus 1981) argues that it's our own internal beliefs, attitudes, interpretations, perceptions, and other factors, in combination with external events in our lives that tend to create stress.

None of the recognised studies include the pressures of social media or a pandemic, so maybe it's time for another study!
Stress is not an illness, but unresolved stress can lead to illness because it drains and weakens the immune system and keeps our bodies on high alert.

PRESSURE V STRESS

It is however important to know the difference between pressure and stress. Pressure is motivating, stimulating, and energising but when it stops us from coping with everyday life, stress is produced.

Most of us can cope with short periods of pressure or mild stress, and it can often be relieved by deep breathing, taking time out to relax, going for a walk, discussing things with friends, or having a good night's sleep. Think of the last time you felt "stressed" – maybe when you were running for a bus, were late for a lecture or had a deadline to meet. As soon as you arrived, or the situation was over, the stress went away. This is pressure, not stress. Continual pressure however can develop into stress. Stress builds up over time; imagine filling a glass of water slowly. When it gets full, it overflows and that's when the trouble starts. The only way that you can put anything else in the glass is by emptying it. See Stress Tips at the end of the chapter.

Chronic (long-term, continuous) stress is much harder to deal with, and can be physically, psychologically, and emotionally damaging, both for you as well as those around you.

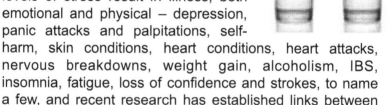

As previously stated, continuous high levels of stress result in illness, both emotional and physical – depression, panic attacks and palpitations, self-harm, skin conditions, heart conditions, heart attacks, nervous breakdowns, weight gain, alcoholism, IBS, insomnia, fatigue, loss of confidence and strokes, to name a few, and recent research has established links between stress and cancer too.

Another glass of water analogy (not half full or half empty!) is the one where a teacher explains that it doesn't matter how heavy the glass of water is, but the longer you hold it for, the heavier it gets until your arm aches and becomes painful.

The traffic light diagram below is a quick and easy way to assess your own stress levels. If you identify with the Green box, your life is pretty much on an even keel, the Amber box indicates continuous pressure and could be a warning sign to take care and assess your lifestyle. The

Red box is self-explanatory – act and make changes before you become ill.

Take a look at the stress tips on the next few pages, you have probably seen them before but how many are you actually implementing? They may seem obvious, but they can make a difference if you are hovering between the green and amber zone. If, however, you are already in the amber zone, you may find the Balance and Control Tips worth considering, stopping you entering the red zone.

The most common stress symptoms are:

irritable moody aches
chest pain headaches
light headed
trembling infections
colds palpitations tense muscles
defensive low energy dizzy
weak bladder frustration
STRESS SYMPTOMS
insomnia carelessness
tiredness easily distracted
poor memory rapid heartbeat
sweating dry mouth
lack of concentration pain
upset stomach temper

It may seem like we are coping, but our nervous systems are still dealing with an overload which can seriously affect our health in the long run. One of the most common physical reactions to stress is the tensing of muscles, which can ultimately trigger tension headaches, migraines, and other musculoskeletal conditions.

Stress is also hard on your digestive system, as it affects which nutrients your intestines absorb. Stress influences how quickly food moves through the body and can provoke us to eat more or less than normal. The disruption of the body's natural digestive processes can cause nausea, pain, vomiting, heartburn, constipation, acid reflux or diarrhoea.

Most of us believe that we should be able to manage our lives without asking for help but when we become overwhelmed or ill as a result, it's time to act.

The Coronavirus pandemic showed us how quickly we could change and adjust our lifestyles. Key workers would have been on high alert all the time and sacrificing sleep which made them vulnerable and more susceptible to the virus.

CONTENTMENT

- No real worries
- Healthy
- Happy
- Sleeping well
- Good friends
- Enjoying life
- Good self-image
- Having fun

GREEN

PRESSURE

- High expectations
- Often Anxious
- Low self esteem
- Outcome driven
- Tense relationships
- People pleaser
- Challenging
- Need to perform

AMBER

STRESS

- Can't cope
- Headaches
- Tense muscles
- Aches and pains
- Poor sleep
- Irritable / moody
- High blood pressure
- Illness

RED

REMEMBER

WHAT is causing you stress?
WHY now?
WHEN did it start?
WHO can you speak to?
WHERE can you go for a change of scene?
HOW are you going to deal with it?

QUICK and EASY STRESS TIPS

- **Drink** *lots of water – keep your body hydrated so you can think clearly*

- **Eat regularly** *- maintain your energy levels*

- **Reduce** *junk foods - sugars and fats can make you sluggish*

- **Exercise** *when you can - bike rides, swimming, dancing, walking*

- **Avoid** excess caffeine intake – (energy drinks and coffee) which can increase feelings of anxiety and agitation

- **Relax** *in a hot bath*

- **Practice** deep breathing – to increase the oxygen to your brain which helps you stay calm

---

QUICK and EASY STRESS TIPS
(continued)

- **Make** *time for yourself to switch off - read, listen to music, watch a film, meditate*

- **Get** *plenty of sleep*

- **Talk** *to someone about your feelings*

- **Never** *be too proud to ask for help*

- **Plan each day** *- structure provides a sense of security*

- **Look** *forward to a night out or a weekend off*

- **Smile** *- release endorphins, the feel-good hormones*

- **Have** *fun with friends and laugh*

- **Keep** *a journal of your thoughts and feelings –better out than in!*

BONUS OFFER
Listen to Stress Relief audio
www.stressworxbooks.com

These may take a little longer to implement but are worth noting.

BALANCE and CONTROL TIPS

Work out, **WHAT** and **WHO** causes you stress, **WHEN** and possibly **WHY** then you can work on **HOW** to manage it.

- **Avoid** *any unnecessary conflict*

- **Have** an attitude of gratitude (be thankful for what you have)

- **Talk** *to someone you trust regularly*

- **Be** *proud when you do something well*

- **Don't** *be too hard on yourself when you make a mistake*

- **Take** *a break from stressful situations*

- **Pace** *yourself*

- **Build** *a network of trusted friends for mutual support*

- **Try** *and plan so you feel in control*

- **Don't** *over commit yourself*

- **Be** *assertive (see **Helpful Stuff**)*

- **Rehearse** *and practice situations that cause you stress (presentations, interviews)*

- **Don't** *over commit or make promises you can't keep*

- **Try** *to reduce excessive eating, drinking, drugs, and smoking*

WHERE DOES STRESS COME FROM?

In Stone Age times, life was straightforward – if you saw a dinosaur, you had the choice of "FIGHT or FLIGHT." Either way, your body would react to the perceived danger by releasing cortisol and adrenaline, which prepares the body for emergency action.

These physical reactions happen very quickly to provide enough energy to fight or run away from the perceived danger.

It does not actually matter if the danger is real or not – our bodies respond the same way each time they sense a threat of some sort.

These are known as the *stress response* which is automatic.

When we *move* into either fight or flight, the hormones produced within the body are used up and the body will then return to normal. (this is where exercise helps) If we "freeze" instead then we do more harm than good because we are unable to escape the stressful situation. The hormones continue to be released, building up within the body which continues to be on high alert and a state of anxiety may come to exist which may lead to those stress related illnesses if not dealt with.

When the cortisol is released – the body automatically responds with
- Increased strength of skeletal muscles
- Decreased blood clotting time
- Increased heart rate
- Increased sugar and fat levels
- Reduced intestinal movement
- Reduced tears and digestive secretions.
- Relaxed bladder
- Dilated pupils
- Increased perspiration
- Increased mental activity
- Low libido
- Inhibited erection/vaginal lubrication
- Constricted blood vessels but dilated in heart, leg, and arm muscles

Despite all the amazing developments in the world since dinosaurs roamed the earth – we still have Stone Age bodies and react in the same way as we did then!

"It's not stress that kills us; it is our reaction to it".
Hans Selye

WHY ARE SOME PEOPLE MORE STRESSED THAN OTHERS?
- Childhood experiences which are reactivated by certain triggers
- Genetics, connected with serotonin levels, the brain's happy hormone
- A weak immune system which makes you more susceptible to stress-related illnesses.
- Lifestyle – poor diet and lack of exercise
- Personality types
- Painful or traumatic memories which create fear
- Bereavement – unable to let go

Different personalities respond and react to situations in different ways. Some people appear to be more anxious than others and worry all the time, and others seem to find life easy and worrying about things is just not in their nature.

WELL KNOWN PERSONALITY TYPES
There are numerous studies on personality types and how they respond to stress but the best known (and simplest) is attributed to Friedman and Rosenman, in the 1950's. They were psychologists who investigated personalities and links to heart attacks. Which are you?

Most of us tend to fall into one category more than the other but depending on circumstances, this can change.

Type A was found to be more susceptible to stress and heart attacks. Which are you? (You can be A/B depending on circumstances)

TYPE A

Often feels under pressure and prone to stress

- Competitive
- Achiever
- Fast worker
- Aggressive
- Impatient
- Hyper-alert
- Explosive speech

TYPE B

Much more laid back

- Relaxed
- Easy going
- Patient
- Not easily irritated
- Time for self
- Mange time well
- Slow and steady attitude
- Not worried about achievement

LESS KNOWN STRESS FACTS

- Stress is linked to the six leading causes of death: heart disease, cancer, lung ailments, accidents, liver cirrhosis, and suicide

- Stress alters the neuro-chemical makeup of the body, which can affect fertility.

- Chronic stress can impair the developmental growth in children by lowering the production of growth hormone from the pituitary gland.

- Chronic stress floods the brain with powerful hormones that are meant for short-term emergency situations. Chronic exposure can damage, shrink, and kill brain cells and is linked to dementia

- Stress can alter blood sugar levels, which can cause mood swings, fatigue, hyperglycaemia, and metabolic syndrome, a major risk factor for heart attack and diabetes.

- Chronic stress decreases the body's immune system's response to infection.

- Studies show that HIV-infected people are more likely to progress to AIDS if they are under high stress than those who are not.

- Post-traumatic stress physically changes children's brains; specifically, stress shrinks the hippocampus, a part of the brain that stores and retrieves memories.

- When cells shrink due to exposure to stress hormones, they disconnect from each other, which contributes to depression.

- Men are more likely than women to develop certain stress-related disorders, including hypertension, aggressive behaviour, and abuse of alcohol and drugs.

In my experience, working with clients and doing talks, understanding *what, why, when,* and *how* stress occurs can be a lightbulb moment.

Andy's wife was expecting their first child and one evening she collapsed, so Andy called an ambulance. When it arrived, he had a panic attack and wanted to hide away to avoid going to the hospital with his wife. He was deeply upset by this and could not understand his reaction which made him feel he had let his wife down. He felt angry with himself and guilty too.

We explored what had happened and then I asked him if he had ever experienced anything similar before. On reflection he recalled that his sister had been rushed to hospital in an ambulance when he was eight years old. Not knowing what was happening, he hid in his bedroom and was scared and shaking. His parents were obviously dealing with his sister's health crisis but failed to explain what was happening to Andy.

As an adult, when he heard the ambulance and saw the blue lights, he went into panic mode, triggered by his childhood memory.
He was delighted to understand why he reacted the way he did. We cleared both memories with EFT (See Tapping Stuff.) and he is now an immensely proud dad of a baby girl.

This example is known as acute stress – when the body reacts or responds to a real or perceived threat to our wellbeing. Chronic stress is ongoing and at the far end of the spectrum, we have Post Traumatic Stress and Burnout.

POST TRAUMATIC STRESS

Trauma is defined as a distressing or disturbing event or experience which can happen to any one of us.

What may seem traumatic to one person, may not be to another. For example, most of us would be upset seeing a badly injured person after a road accident but this is a regular occurrence for paramedics, fire fighters, police officers, doctors and nurses. It used to be known as shell shock and was only thought to be suffered by soldiers after the traumas of war.

So, what classes as a traumatic event?
- Serious accidents – either experienced first-hand or witnessed
- Loss of a loved one – sudden death, murder
- Physical or sexual assault and rape
- Emotional and physical abuse including childhood, sexual and domestic abuse
- Involvement in a natural disaster
- A global pandemic
- Serious health problems – failed operations, amputations, terminal illness
- Loss of a child
- War
- Torture

When a traumatic event occurs, part of the brain shuts down to protect us and this prevents us from processing what is going on around us. This is what makes us feel numb and detached from reality.

PTSD can cause flashbacks, nightmares, repetitive and distressing physical responses such as panic, fear, anger and the general stress response.

Some people manage to overcome traumatic incidents quite quickly, but others are haunted for many years afterwards and their mental and physical health suffers.

Incidents that happen in childhood can affect us for the rest of our lives unless they are laid to rest with therapy.

It does not matter how old we are, traumatic incidents can haunt us for a long, long time.

Having recently visited Auschwitz and Birkenau, I really can't comprehend the ongoing trauma and horrors that prisoners were subjected to during the Holocaust.

One survivor was Viktor Emil Frankl who was an Austrian neurologist and psychiatrist. He survived Theresienstadt, Auschwitz, Kaufering and Türkheim.

"Those who have a 'why' to live, can bear with almost any 'how'."

"When we are no longer able to change a situation, we are challenged to change ourselves."

Viktor E. Frankl

No matter how extreme the objective reality, we always have a choice in how we deal with it. This may mean working through ways in managing the situation or ending it, by committing suicide.

Our minds record everyday events and experiences and recalling them does not cause any discomfort. However, when we have flashbacks of uncomfortable or scary memories, we do whatever we can to make them go away.

We try to avoid being reminded by staying away from people and places that act as a trigger to recall the incident.

We may also avoid talking about it because that makes us relive it, so it is easier to distract ourselves by keeping busy and withdrawing from people who we assume would not understand as they haven't had the same experience.

It is unlikely that the traumatic event will happen again but that does not stop the fear that it will. Many PTSD sufferers are constantly anxious and on edge. They are easily startled and prone to be irritable, have anger issues and struggle to concentrate.

Others lose their hair or go grey prematurely or try to "make it go away" with drug or alcohol abuse. They tend to push people close to them away which often results in isolation and loneliness, causing relationship breakdowns.

Suppressed traumas can manifest themselves into all sorts of physical illnesses and conditions.

Mike came to see me with anger issues – things came to a head when he found himself about to shake his partners 4-year-old autistic son whose behaviour triggered an anger that Mike could not control. He didn't understand what happened to trigger this, but his partner left him saying that she wasn't prepared to put up with it any longer. As she was carrying Mike's child, this was the tipping point for him to do something about it. His mum (a previous client) came with him for the first session. I asked him when he became aware of his anger and his mum asked him if he thought that the accident had anything to do with it.

When Mike was 17, he was with his friend Alex one Sunday evening at a friend's house. They left to cross the road to Mike's car. It was dark and Alex stepped into the road a split second before Mike and was hit by a speeding car. Mike was helpless to stop Alex flying into the air and landing on the road.

He went into automatic and ran to a house and was knocking on the door and shouting for help. The ambulance came after neighbours tried to do CPR on Alex, but it was too late. Mike remembered trying to keep the traffic away from the accident, in total shock, frozen by what had just happened. He recalls picking up Alex's shoe and sobbing, then his dad arriving at the scene and he recalls being hugged tightly. Sadly, Alex's mum had lost her husband the year before and Alex was her only child.

His anger was mainly directed at himself. After the accident he had to give evidence at the inquest, and he gave an economic version of what happened because his friends mum was there too, and Mike didn't want to add to her grief.

I was quickly able to join up the dots – he had developed a pattern of self-blame for a range of things that had happened since. His anger was towards himself for not preventing the accident. He was riddled with guilt and tortured himself with "If only". He had not realised the impact of this experience and subsequently became involved in an abusive relationship where he was physically abused but blamed himself.

He began to see the links himself and quickly made progress with EFT and Hypnosis. The memory stopped haunting him and his anger pattern dissolved, He is planning to go and see Alex's mum, which is another guilt he was carrying. Because he blamed himself, he couldn't face his mum, assuming that she blamed him too.
We worked through the memories and then Mike started to have panic attacks as the shock and horror resurfaced- like a movie in his mind that he had blocked for so long. He could hear the sounds and see himself standing by the ambulance holding his friend's shoe in total shock and disbelief.

Slowly and surely, he began to heal and as his girlfriend started to see the evidence of his change, she gave him another chance. They have subsequently settled into family life with their new baby son - called Alex.

BURNOUT

Burnout is the result of mental, physical, and emotional exhaustion due to ongoing demands, pressures, and expectations. It is generally considered to be work related, but others can suffer too. Good examples are

carers or family members looking after someone with a severe disability or dementia with no support.

Burnout is defined by the World Health Organisation as an official syndrome related to "chronic workplace stress that has not been successfully managed."

This definition was certainly applicable during lockdown for frontline workers who were working and living with continual stress, exhaustion, and fear. Can students burnout? Of course!

Causes of Burnout

In a nutshell – priorities, processes, personalities, pessimism, perfectionism, and pressures all contribute to burnout as well as lack of purpose.

- **Priorities** – which are not your own can cause stress especially if they are not in line with your value system.
- **Pressures** - high expectations to meet deadlines which can impact on others plus unmanageable workloads
- **Personalities** - personality A is more likely to suffer from burnout than personality B. Personality clashes and dominant personalities in authority do not help!
- **Professionalism** - (lack of) from fellow students and tutors with limited guidance and support.
- **Processes** - lack of clarity on roles and responsibilities
- **Perfectionism** - feeling inadequate can be a driver to do more and more to prove that you are good enough (or better)

- **Productivity** - poor time management and low energy prevents completion of tasks.
- **Pessimism** - a negative environment and culture
- **Planning** - not having a clear study plan and / or personal development plan can contribute to burnout.
- **Performance** - no work life balance (Poor planning prevents performance)
- **Purpose** – where are you heading after your qualification?

What to look for:

BURNOUT PREVENTION TIPS

- **Plan** *each day carefully and try to stick to it*

- **Keep** *an eye on your time management*

- **Work** *your planned hours as far as possible*

- **Write** a *"To do list" every day and prioritise tasks*

- **Set** *clear boundaries*

- **Work** *to your deadlines*

- **Learn** to say no without feeling guilty

- **Keep** *your tutor up to speed if you are not coping*

- **Share** *personal things that may be holding you back*

- **Ask** *for extra support if needed*

- **Take** *regular breaks from your computer*

- **Have** *a lunch break every day and get some fresh air*

- **Learn** *EFT to release stress as it arises (See* **Tapping Stuff***)*

- **Keep** *weekends free for social activities*

- **Don't** *procrastinate – Just Do It!*

- **Avoid** *working all night*

- **Get** *enough sleep*

Exam Stress

One of the major causes of stress at university, is of course exams. Whether you are a Fresher or in your final year, you want to do well and get a good degree.

Exam nerves are perfectly normal and range, from a mild nervousness to full panic. They often start with tests at primary school and develop through to GCSEs and A levels and any subsequent exams if not dealt with.

Exam stress is:
• Excessive worry about not doing enough revision
• Fear of failure and the consequences of poor results
• Anxiety about friends doing better than you
• Worrying about letting your family and yourself down
• Negative beliefs about your ability
• Self-doubt
• Procrastination
• Feeling out of control and panicky
• Feeling overwhelmed by worry

Stress, tension, and worry can stop us sleeping, which obviously makes us tired, making us unable to concentrate, and the cycle continues.

We never quite know what to expect or what is expected of us at exam time, but when and how does it tip over into ongoing anxiety and stress which is debilitating?

Exams are a means to an end; they are not the be all and end all. See Tips for Revision and Exams in **Challenging Stuff** and how to deal with nerves in **Tapping Stuff**

3
MIND
STUFF

This chapter explores and explains how the mind works. Some people who are stressed, just accept how they feel (whilst it is manageable), but others choose to do something about it.

It takes courage to tell a therapist what is going on and how they feel. One of the most common things I hear is "It sounds really silly". Their perception is that they are the only ones with their problem and cannot understand why they can't deal with it themselves. Seeking help is usually the last resort.

We all try to make sense of things in our lives, but often rational thought doesn't give us the answers we need.
Feeling scared, having an unwanted habit, being haunted by negative memories, or limiting beliefs is not going to be resolved without understanding what, why and how these feelings came about and the effect they have on our lives.
When clients come to see me, they tell me about their stress over a cuppa. When I give them a simple explanation of how the subconscious mind works and why they feel the way they do, they feel relieved, less tense, more relaxed, have a different perspective and feel hopeful that their situation is resolvable.

Our minds are the most powerful computers that we will ever come across – they add and delete, save, and rename files and are even subject to virus attacks which can grind things to a halt.

Our memories are like those of the computer – they store everything that happens to us – good bad and indifferent. The memory is non-judgemental but not always accurate. It is part of the subconscious mind as are our imaginations together with our established behaviour patterns and automatic body functions. The subconscious mind controls our heartbeat, the pumping of our lungs, blood flow, the digestive system and so on. Just imagine having to **think** about breathing, swallowing, or blinking – we wouldn't last long at all!

Have a look at these Russian dolls, each one fits into the next one, representing each stage of life

| 1 | 2 | 3 | 4 | 5 |

1. Early childhood
2. Adolescence
3. Adulthood
4. Middle age
5. Old age

Everything that happens to us on our life journey is recorded in our minds and taken to the next stage. It does not actually matter when a problem starts, be it in early childhood or later. Everything is stored in the same way in the subconscious part of the mind which is like a computer or filing cabinet. All our automatic body functions, memories, beliefs, values, fears, habits, behaviour patterns and early messages are retained for automatic recall when triggered by circumstances.

If you can remember learning your tables, spellings, riding a bike or learning to drive, – it took repetition and practice before the learning moved from your conscious mind to the subconscious where it was filed away until you needed it.

Do you find that if you are with a young child, you are surprised that you can remember fairy stories and nursery rhymes easily, even though you haven't thought about them for years? Another good example is when you hear a song that you liked when you were younger – you immediately recall the words! Do you know what 6 x 6 is without having to go through the whole table? You are not thinking about these things until they are triggered by the situation you are in and then your subconscious gives you the answer, when you need it.

With computer files or a filing cabinet, when everything is in order and in the correct place, it is easy to find what you are looking for – our lives, however, are rarely so organised and often things get mixed up and stored in the wrong place or hidden from view!

Our minds also get cluttered up with rubbish and viruses which cause us distress, tension, anxiety, and depression as well as bad habits, fears and phobias – all that negativity that we want to be rid of. Is it time for a clear out?

A person who is scared or lacks confidence giving presentations or public speaking will undoubtedly have a painful or embarrassing memory (usually at school) when he or she pronounced a word wrongly, tripped over or stammered and everyone laughed or commented. All those feelings come back as soon as you think about standing up and speaking in front of others.

You may have forgotten the original event consciously, but your subconscious certainly has not and will give you all those feelings back again! The more it happens, of course, the worse the problem seems to be.
Sadly, the subconscious is unaware of the difference between right and wrong, fact or fiction, and gives us back

what we gave it. If you learned a spelling incorrectly or you learned that 6x6 was 35 instead of 36 then that is what you will receive as an answer when you are asked what 6 x 6 is!

Once we have trained our subconscious mind to do certain tasks, we trust it to get on with it without having to think about it at all.
The subconscious mind never sleeps and is always busy keeping us going like well-oiled machinery and is often in conflict with the conscious mind which is an exceedingly small percentage (approximately 5%) of our brain power. (The here and now and rational thought.) It is subject to overload and needs to be recharged with sleep.

When we have had a stressful day or have troubles then it is often hard to switch off, and sleep becomes difficult and sometimes impossible. The conscious mind will not shut down. Loss of sleep, as we all know, makes it harder to function and the stress levels increase.
No matter what we *do, think,* or *know,* if we don't *feel* right, anxiety, discomfort and stress can develop.

Emotions and Thoughts
Emotions are triggered by our thoughts and they affect the way we behave and live our lives.

Emotional health is probably far harder to understand than physical and cognitive (thinking brain) development.
Positive emotions help us to believe in ourselves, have a positive attitude and be confident with high self-esteem, self-respect and self-worth.

Those with positive emotions are far more likely to:
• Have peace of mind
• Enjoy their lives
• Be able to laugh and have fun
• Be able to deal with stress and recover from tough times
• Have a sense of purpose and, or direction in their lives
• Attract other positive people into their lives

- Be open minded to learn new things in life
- Be open to and welcome change
- Develop a balance between work and play.
- Make and sustain good relationships
- Have self-confidence and high self-esteem

Being positive emotionally does not mean that life is plain sailing or that we will not experience negative emotions and setbacks, but it does mean that we are stronger and more able to cope with the tough times.

There are hundreds of labels that we give to our feelings, which are, by degree, positive or negative.
Humans have a natural tendency to move from pain to pleasure, but of course, we need to know how!

Negative emotions can take over and control our lives (if we let them) resulting in life being an uphill struggle. Would you rather feel sad or glad? In control or feeling overwhelmed? No-one wants to feel bad all the time, but it can become a pattern or habit if we are not careful.

Some people find it hard to identify what they are feeling and do not recognise the difference between thoughts and feelings.

Here is a lovely parable, which illustrates the point.
An old Cherokee is teaching his grandson about life. "A fight goes on inside us all" he said to the boy.
"It is a terrible fight, and it is between two wolves. One is evil – he is anger, envy, sorrow, regret, greed, arrogance, self-pity, guilt, resentment, inferiority, lies, false pride, superiority, and ego." He continued, "The other is good – he is joy, peace, love, hope, serenity, humility, kindness, benevolence, empathy, generosity, truth, compassion, and faith."

The grandson thought about it for a minute and then asked his grandfather, "Which wolf wins?" The old Cherokee simply replied, "The one you feed."
Which wolf do you feed?

Attitudes Beliefs and Values

The obvious question that we all ask ourselves is "Where do my feelings come from?" "Why do I feel negative, miserable, stressed, and useless when friends and people around us are positive, in control and enjoying life?"

The answer lies in how we have trained our minds, which includes our attitudes, beliefs and values which contribute to how we feel and see the world

Attitudes - are feelings that we have towards something or someone else, which can be positive or negative. Would your attitude to your friend change if you found him/her stealing from you or if you discovered that your neighbour was a paedophile or a murderer?

Beliefs - are ideas that are accepted as truth and certainty Beliefs have the power to: Create (Empowering) or Destroy (Limiting)

Most of us have inherited beliefs from childhood and accept them as gospel, probably unaware that these may only one perspective or interpretation.

Like attitudes, beliefs can be changed by circumstances, e.g. loss of faith in God after personal tragedy, or by evidence. For example, in 1954 Roger Bannister believed he could run a mile in under 4 minutes. That may seem slow to us now compared to Usain Bolt, but he was a world record breaker when he did it in 3 min 59.4 seconds. We used to believe that the world was flat until explorers and scientists provided *evidence* that proved that it is round.

Thirty years ago, no-one would have believed that we would have phones in our pockets and be able to connect to the internet anywhere in the world in seconds!
Who would have believed that Covid-19 could spread so quickly, kill so many and have such an impact on our lives?

Global beliefs are almost indisputable as there is so much evidence to reinforce them.

54

Religious beliefs and **personal** beliefs tend to be either positive or negative.

Negative (limiting) beliefs that we hold about ourselves can cause stress, low self-esteem, and lack of confidence.
If all our beliefs were positive, life would be much easier!
The most common limiting belief I come across with clients is "not being good enough" and this can influence every aspect of life.

I was knocked down by a car when I was three and apart from a scar on my nose, there didn't appear to be any other damage. However, I managed to fracture both ears which resulted in nerve damage and deafness. I couldn't understand why I missed things or felt lost at school and it took the medics (and my parents fighting for me) until I was eight before my deafness was acknowledged. I was given a hearing aid which was horrid, and I was easy pickings for teasing. I was a borderline pass for the 11+ which entitled me to an interview, but I was told that I couldn't possibly cope with grammar school – why? Because I was deaf.

The seeds were sown for my negative belief – I was deaf and therefore daft. Despite my mum going out to work to pay for a private grammar school education, those seeds grew. I blew my GCSE's, only getting two out of nine. I managed to get enough retakes to get to teachers training college, but it wasn't until I did a diploma in counselling skills that my negative belief started to shift. I had some counselling myself as a requirement of the course and explored all the memories and the impact of them, relating to my hearing loss. After this I could wear my hearing aids and went on to be the Head of the Youth Service in a London Borough, a tutor for youth work training at Brunel and then the Chairperson of The Centre for Youth Work Studies, and an Ofsted Inspector as well. My belief didn't change however until I got my Masters degree in Counselling Psychology when I had the evidence that maybe I wasn't so daft after all!

Values

Do you know your shoe size? Of course, you do! What about your core values?
Which is more important?!

Our values are the things that we believe to be important in the way we live our lives, both at home and work. They are usually formed early on in life and are often accepted as a framework for living.

Most of us accept that stealing is wrong, and that alone stops us from even thinking about it, let alone doing it!
Our early values are called "received values" because they are received from parents, grandparents, extended family, and teachers who shape our early lives. At an early age we don't really know anything different from the way we are taught, either literally or by example.

However, in teenage years, we accept, reject or test those values until we are comfortable with what is *really* important to us. They can of course change – if you are driven by career and income but then marry and have a family, whilst your career is still important to you, it's not as important as it was before the patter of tiny feet.

Values are a personal hidden agenda which helps us to determine our priorities, choose our friends, where we shop, or go on holiday. They are the measures we use to make decisions and choices.

Have a look at the values below, and see which ones immediately resonate with you.

Now think about your top ten values – are they aligned with your perception of yourself?

These are your **CORE** values.
• Do they make you feel good about yourself?
• Are they representative of the life you lead?
• Do they inform your decision-making and choices in life?

Now think about those you are closest to, friends and family. You will probably find that these people have similar values to yourself and those you do not get on with so well have different values to you. Student years often determine our life-long values – late night debates or disputes about putting the world to rights and discovering how others think and feel.

Many relationship breakdowns are caused by diverse value systems which are harder to change than beliefs and attitudes. Conflicting values cause stress!

Perceptions

Look at your fingerprint – it is different from anyone else's in the world! There may be some similarities, but you are unique. In the same way, our perceptions, or how we see the world, are unique to each of us.

We all see things in different ways and at different times. We learn at different paces and in different ways – some of us learn better by seeing things, others by listening and others by doing.

Look at the pictures below. What do you see first, the vase or the two faces? There are two ways of perceiving the same picture.

What about this next one? It's a sign that you have probably seen loads of times, but have you really *seen* it?

Yes, it's the FEDEX logo. Can you see the arrow? Have you noticed it before? Most people get caught out with this one.

Can you see the white arrow between the E and X? Maybe you can now but why have you not seen it before? It's always been there! You were probably not expecting to see it, but you will always see it in future!

If our perceptions of ourselves are negative because of negative messages, discrimination, bullying, lack of support, etc., then the result is low self-esteem, lack of confidence, insecurity, feeling vulnerable, powerless, unlovable, and unable to change.

By looking at something differently, we send a new signal to our brains, allowing us to perceive things in more than one way.

Many of us often accept our first impressions of people, situations, and feelings without checking to see if there is another way of looking at things. It is always worth checking out that these impressions or perceptions are correct.

Jim believed that his parents had always loved his brother more than him, and his evidence was that his brother asked for a razor at 16 and got one. Jim waited patiently for his 16th birthday but did not receive a razor (which meant, in his eyes he was accepted as a man). No razor at Christmas either – he never got one and for all his adult life this affected him, and he believed he was unlovable. He never actually asked his parents for a razor as a present! At the age of 74, he started to see things from another perspective.

By being more self-aware, and checking our assumptions, we can avoid some of the pickles we get ourselves into!

This applies to stereotypes too. This is a fixed idea that we have about people, usually from either our perceptions or those of others. For example, as a child you were probably told that if you got lost or were in trouble, you should ask a policeman. However, as you got older, your perception of the police might have changed because of experiences you or friends may have had. Society tends to stereotype, usually negatively and often in relation to minorities and based on assumptions.

We become so used to negative patterns of thinking and feeling that they seem reasonable, normal, and justified, and we no longer notice the effect they are having on us. No matter how bad or untrue the thoughts are, we tend to *believe* them. This is very painful to live with, and unless we take positive steps to change our thinking habits, those negative thoughts and feelings will always be with us and dominate our minds.

"Think you can, think you can't; either way you'll be right."
Henry Ford

If we kept a record (who does?!!), we may have noticed a pattern to our negative thinking. Looking back, do you still hold on to negative thinking habits from childhood or teenage years? Have they become limiting beliefs? Check them out! Where is your evidence that your beliefs are correct?

The price we pay for negative beliefs is remarkably high, as I discovered for myself, and I see many adults who are victims of their past.

Remember the saying "Laugh and the world laughs with you, cry and you cry alone." Try and be with positive people, not negative ones as they will get you down.

"If you believe you can, you are halfway there".
Teddy Roosevelt

Negative Beliefs can be changed **– see Tapping Stuff**

The subconscious mind is also responsible for sad or bad memories or experiences.

These are stored in your subconscious, as are happy and joyful memories. Happy memories stimulate and trigger-happy feelings whilst sad or bad memories trigger sad and upsetting emotions, which cause stress. Any similar circumstance to the original event will trigger those feelings again – your subconscious thinks you want those feelings back, so it gives them to you without you asking or giving "permission!" As you saw in the last chapter, traumatic events linger for years and cause so much damage. What you had for lunch three weeks ago is irrelevant so its not stored but significant impactful memories are. You may remember what you need for your exams in the short term but it's unlikely you will recall this information in ten years' time!

THE MONKEY ON YOUR SHOULDER

Is there a little voice inside you telling you that your negative thoughts, feelings, attitudes, doubts, fears, and beliefs are true or justified? This is your monkey!

"Monkeys" are worries, negative beliefs, doubts, messages, fears, habits, thoughts, and feelings that never keep quiet and refuse to sit still. They just will not leave us alone, however much we tell them to. They are the automatic patterns of thoughts and feelings that are caged in our heads. Monkeys are what prevent us from thinking clearly, reaching our goals, and feeling more peaceful and positive about ourselves.

Monkeys love the word **SHOULD** – do you recognise these?

I *should* be nice to everyone
I *should* work hard all the time
I *should* be successful
I *should* do things perfectly
I *should* lose weight
I *should* eat healthy food
I *should* always look good
I *should* have a boyfriend/girlfriend/partner
I *should* feel confident in every situation
I *should* set goals and targets
I *should* always say the right things at the right time
I *should* always feel calm and in control

I *should* be happy
I *should* never make mistakes
I *should* put other people's needs before my own
I *should* never say anything that might make other people feel uncomfortable
I *should* always make the right decisions
I *should* exercise regularly
I *should* get a good degree

Who is in control – you or your monkey?
Change the word **should** to **could** and see how that feels!

HABITS AND ADDICTIONS

Einstein said, "The *definition of insanity is doing the same thing over and over again and expecting different results.*"
We must all be insane because we all have habits, some good and some bad, which we may try to change, or we may be happy with them because they serve a purpose.
Habits or behaviour patterns are initially developed at an early age, and it is generally believed that it only takes 21 days to create a habit.

Ask someone close to you what habits s/he thinks you have, as you may be unaware of them. Habits can become so much a part of us that it may come as a surprise to have them pointed out! They become an integral part of us through repetition and practice which is not always deliberate.

As children we copy and learn behaviour patterns from parents or family, and sometimes develop habits to meet a need for comfort or reassurance, such as needing a dummy, comfort blanket, or thumb sucking.

We usually grow out of early habits naturally, but the more we practice these behaviour patterns the stronger they become. We cease to think or be aware of what we are doing. Think about learning to ride a bike, roller skate, swim, read, or learning tables.... At first it feels almost impossible, but with repetition and lots of practice it suddenly all seems to come together and become automatic. Learning to drive is another good example. This is because the repetition and practice become consolidated and moves from the "thinking" part of your mind (the conscious) to the automatic part (subconscious). Most of our habits are not harmful or damaging to our lifestyle or to others, but sometimes they become annoying and need to be broken.

Substance abuse and alcohol usage and habits increased during lockdown by more than a third. This book touches on drug usage in **Health Stuff** but the subject is so vast and controversial; I am leaving it well alone.

Sometimes willpower is enough to break these patterns, but it needs to be extraordinarily strong because willpower is part of the conscious mind and is usually overpowered by the subconscious.

Habits can be broken! – **See Tapping Stuff**

"I stopped biting my nails with EFT – after 65 years! I am amazed. Thanks Ruth!" Diana. Portsmouth

ADDICTION

A habit turns into an addiction when you are aware that you "need" the item to get through daily living and feel out of control and panicky without it.

Common addictions include alcohol, drugs, smoking, gambling, computer games, internet trawling (phone, tablet etc) social media, shopping, food and chocolate.

There is no single reason why addictions develop. Addictions to substances change the way we feel, both mentally and physically. If the experience is a good one, then there may be a strong desire or need to repeat it. This also applies to gambling and the "high" of winning, which almost brainwashes us against the odds and the realties or fears of losing.

A good way of checking if you have a habit or addiction is to ask yourself to what degree you could do without this behaviour or substance. The stronger the need, the more likely it is to be an addiction.

When we hear the word addiction, we tend to think of substances, sex and gambling, but exercise and gaming have been acknowledged as addictions too. Arguably, we can become addicted to any behaviour that is persistent, in search of some form of gratification. If they make us feel better in some way – provide a buzz, relaxation, or escapism, then we tend to go back to them. The brain's chemistry starts to adapt, demanding more until the body becomes dependent and unpleasant withdrawal symptoms are avoided.

What to look for: (signs and symptoms vary according to the addiction)
• Extreme mood changes – happy, sad, excited, anxious,
• Sleeping a lot more or less than usual, or at different times of day or night
• Changes in energy – unexpectedly and extremely tired or energetic

- Weight loss or weight gain
- Unexpected and persistent coughs or sniffles
- Health swings from well to unwell for no obvious reason
- Pupils of the eyes seeming smaller or larger than usual
- Unusual secretiveness
- Uncharacteristic lying
- Stealing
- Financially unpredictable – flush or broke
- Changes in social groups
- Repeated unexplained outings, often with a sense of urgency
- Drug paraphernalia such as unusual pipes, cigarette papers, small weighing scales,
- "Stashes" of drugs, often in small plastic, paper or foil packages

NB – Don't jump to conclusions!

HOARDING

As an ex primary teacher, I thought I was something of a hoarder, saving egg and match boxes, lollipop sticks and whatever else I could lay my hands on for art and craft lessons. However, I had no emotional attachment to these things and was happy to share with my class. On reflection, I was just diligent!
It is unlikely that many students have the space to hoard stuff but it's worth knowing about.

Hoarding was confirmed as a mental health condition in 2018 and is described as a difficulty in letting go of or discarding possessions. The thought of disposing of things triggers stress, anxiety and resistance.
Some people hoard things that they were deprived of in childhood, others keep things "just in case" or for a rainy day. So how can you tell if someone is suffering from hoarding disorder?

Look out for those who are:
- Holding onto things that are not needed

- Being upset at the thought of disposing of "stuff", regardless of its value
- Resistant to throwing things out
- Feeling unsafe without their clutter
- Building up of "stuff" to the point where rooms become unusable or unsafe
- Possessive of items, such as newspapers, clothes, paperwork, books or sentimental items like birthday cards
- Unaware that there is a problem
- Aggressive with anyone who tries to dispose of the "junk"
- Convinced that their "stuff" will be needed one day
- Not wanting to waste anything

Hoarding disorder is different from collecting. A collector of things like stamps or china has an attachment to them but not in a possessive way that can cause distress or anxiety.

You can check how much of a hoarder you are by using the Clutter Image Rating **www.hoardingdisordersuk.org/research-and-resources/clutter-image-ratings**

FEARS AND PHOBIAS

Fear can be described in different terms in relation to the degree of fear that is experienced. This varies from mild caution to extreme phobia and paranoia, with anxiety, worry, terror, horror, panic, and dread falling between the extremes.

Being afraid of something that can cause harm is a normal reaction. However, some people show strong, persistent, and irrational fears of objects, activities, or situations. When this behaviour interferes with normal everyday functioning, the condition is called a phobia.

It could be argued that FEAR stands for **F**antasies **E**xperienced **A**s **R**eal. This is because the subconscious mind cannot differentiate between what is real and what is imagined.

For example, a fear of spiders can be reactivated just by thinking of one, even though there isn't one in sight. However, the mind will trigger the fear based on the original experience and response.

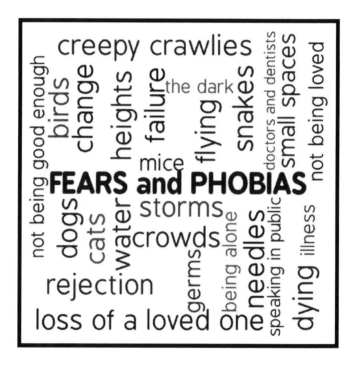

We become used to our fears and generally try to avoid them; e.g. if you are scared of flying then you travel by train or boat, or if you have a fear of heights, you stay at ground level. When confronted with a fear, your body automatically goes into the stress response.
• Trembling or shaking

- Feeling of choking
- Sweating
- Nausea /sickness feeling
- Palpitations, pounding heart
- Chest pain or discomfort
- Feeling unsteady, dizzy, light-headed, or faint
- Feelings of unreality or of being detached from yourself
- Fear of losing control or going crazy

See **Tapping Stuff** to release your fears.

Pam came to see me with a fear of flying, as she was due to fly within two weeks; she was becoming more and more anxious. The fear had materialised a few years ago after a close friend died abroad.

The real issue was the trauma and grief that the death had caused which had not been cleared. Pam was very close to the family and was supporting her friend's mum. To do this, she felt she had to remain strong and she kept busy arranging the funeral and contacting people. After that, she sorted clothes and possessions to feel close to her friend. She was scared that if she went abroad, that she would die too.

This manifested itself into a fear of flying. By tapping gently on the grief, the memories and the pain her fears dissolved, and she enjoyed a well-deserved rest on holiday.

***

Mia was eight years old and she was terrified of dogs. Every time she saw one, she panicked and cried. Her three sisters were keen to get a dog, but it wasn't possible with Mia's fear.

We tapped for the fear first and it came down a bit but not enough for her to feel comfortable. Eventually after her mum tried to remember any incidents that involved dogs, she recalled an incident in a park. Mia was in the back seat of the car and as her dad leant over her to undo her seat belt, a dog jumped into the car and onto Mia's lap! The shock and fear were so much for the little girl that she blocked the memory. Even though she couldn't really remember this incident, we worked on how it must have felt, and she imagined a dog jumping on her. After a few rounds she felt better and now she is much more comfortable around dogs. The family is now planning on getting a puppy, with Mia's blessing.

***

Jane had a spider phobia and unfortunately for her, she was a manager of a family business which was a paper factory which was overrun with spiders!

When she left after her session, she acknowledged that she felt different but could not believe that her phobia had gone. I stated that she would know as soon as she saw a spider and thought no more about it. Two weeks later, I received an email – Jane had watched the film Arachnophobia, and was fine, she had put a picture of a Black Widow spider on her fridge, and was fine and then she went to the Tarantula House at Longleat House to prove to herself that her phobia had gone!

NEEDS AND WANTS

We all have needs, both physical and emotional. Emotional needs are by degree and can change with circumstances. Physical needs are more straightforward in that we know when we are hungry, tired, or cold without doubt, and we know that we usually meet these needs with food, sleep or warmth.

Emotional needs are harder to identify but most of us can relate to them.

How do we work out what is a need and what is a want?
We may *need* a new pair of shoes because our old ones had worn out, but we do not *need* the latest fashion or loads of pairs – we *want* them!

You have probably come across Maslow's hierarchy of needs, do you agree that the pandemic has made the top two tiers almost redundant whilst we focus on the three lower ones?

CONTROL

One thing we all want, and need is to feel in control of our thoughts, and feelings. The Pandemic has sadly taken much of that control away. However, there are things that we are still in control of. Steven Covey talks about Circles of Control, Influence and Concern. (The 7 Habits of Highly Effective People)

The Circle of Concern represents what we worry about but have no control over, like the weather, the virus, our skin colour and height..

"If there is no solution to the problem then don't waste time worrying about it. If there is a solution to the problem, then don't waste time worrying about it."
The Dalai Lama

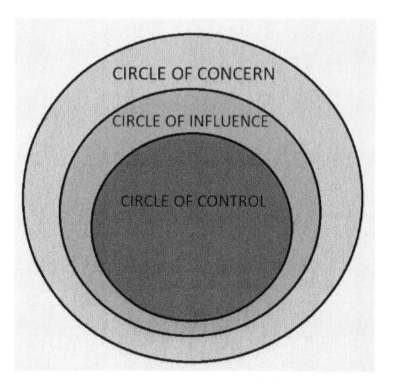

The first habit is "Be Proactive" and the Circle of Influence is relevant to proactive people who take responsibility for their lives. They recognise that no-one else is going to do it! What or who influences you? Who do you or who could you influence? We are not talking about brain washing here but a sensible approach to things that you may be able to change through dialogue, discussion, challenge, and negotiation. A good example is challenging discriminatory comments.

What others say or do is outside your direct control but you may be able to influence a situation.
You can increase your circle of influence by:

- Being a good listener. - build trust and rapport
- Being consistent - reliable and responsive
- Showing empathy - relate to the experiences and feelings of others
- Finding solutions - practical ideas to move things forward
- Accepting responsibility for your actions – not blaming anyone else
- Appreciating and valuing others - They will remember!
- Having a vision or goal that others can relate to
- Being passionate and enthusiastic - it's magnetic
- Keeping well informed

What or who influences you? Your friends, family, your course, social media? TV?

What is within your circle of control? What do you have control of in your life? How many of the following would you place in your circle of control?
- Your beliefs
- Your values
- Your attitudes
- Who your friends are
- What you eat
- What you read
- How much you drink / smoke. / take drugs
- Which courses you do
- How hard you work
- How honest you are
- How much exercise you do
- How you spend your money
- How kind you are
- How often you say thank you
- How much you smile / laugh
- What risks you take
- How responsible and trustworthy you are

I am sure there are others, but we all have more control of our lives than perhaps we realise.

MEMORIES

The phrase "making memories" prompts thoughts of good times that we have enjoyed with friends or family. Happy memories generate happy feelings, but painful or uncomfortable memories trigger painful and uncomfortable feelings. As you have seen, traumatic memories become embedded in the subconscious mind along with impact of that memory. Any similar experience will bring back the emotions that the first event caused.

Everything starts somewhere and when we can track back to the start point, subsequent emotions and behaviour patterns become more understandable and can be worked on.

A good technique to reduce the impact of a painful memory is to imagine that you are sitting in a cinema, watching the memory on the screen. You have a remote control beside you, so you press play, see the colours, and hear the sounds and when the "film" reaches the end, press rewind and watch it backwards. Press play again but this time imagine it in black and white. You will find that the intensity the memory and the emotional attachment will fade.

Reduce the impact of uncomfortable or painful memories in **Tapping Stuff**

The rest of this chapter is focused on Mental Health to increase awareness and dispel myths.

MENTAL HEALTH

Sadly, since the beginning of the NHS in 1948 physical and mental health care have been perceived as separate issues. When we have a physical health problem, we do not hesitate to seek medical advice but in most cases, a mental health professional is only consulted when there is a crisis, or someone is desperate for help.

Mental or emotional health is key to your psychological wellbeing and plays a major role in maintaining physical health.

We all have mental health and in the same way as we have days when we don't feel too good physically, we can all have "bad days" emotionally too. That does not mean that we have a mental illness or a mental health condition.
Good mental health is not about feeling happy and confident 24/7 and ignoring challenges, it is about coping effectively and realistically with life.

A mental illness or mental health condition is diagnosable but can be scary – for the person experiencing it as well as for friends, families, colleagues, and employers who may not know how to help.

The definition of mental illness is "a condition which causes serious disorder in a person's behaviour or thinking."
The MIND website has a comprehensive A-Z of mental health issues and conditions.
www.mind.org.uk/information-support/types-of-mental-health-problems

There are far too many to go into here, so the focus is on the most common conditions, a quick mention on others with references or links for more information.
The continuum starting from a happy and healthy mind to an unhappy and unhealthy mind is usually a long one, with numerous circumstances along the way.
Not every mental health condition can be attributed to stress, but like physical health, all mental health issues can be worsened or intensified by stress and tension.

1 in 4 ADULTS IN THE UK EXPERIENCE A MENTAL HEALTH PROBLEM EACH YEAR.

• Depression	3 in 100
• Anxiety	4.7 in 100
• Mixed anxiety and depression	9.7 in 100
• OCD	1.3 in 100
• Panic disorder	1.2 in 100

These numbers were pre pandemic. The ONS (Office for National Statistics) has carried out surveys throughout lockdown and in April 2020.

• 75% of those asked were worried about the future,
• 62.7% stated that they were anxious and stressed,
• 36.1% were feeling lonely,
• 30.5% said that the pandemic made their mental health worse
• and 10.4% said that they had no-one to talk to about their anxieties.

ANXIETY

This is a persistent feeling of unease, worry or fear and like stress, has physical symptoms:
• A sense of dread
• Feeling on edge
• Irritable
• Dizziness
• Heart palpitations
• Breathlessness
• Dry mouth
• Headaches

It is quite normal to feel anxious or worried about an exam, operation, interview, or a new situation but when these cause distress on a regular basis, you may be suffering from a diagnosable anxiety disorder.

These are categorised as:
• General Anxiety Disorder (as above)
• Panic Disorder

- Post Traumatic Disorder (See **Stress Stuff**)
- Social anxiety disorder
- Obsessive Compulsive Disorder
- Phobias (See previous pages)

PANIC DISORDER

Panic disorder is where you have regular panic attacks, often for no apparent reason that you can identify. Most panic attacks result from a sudden overwhelming sense of intense fear or discomfort. Severe stress, a shock, such as the sudden death of a loved one, divorce, or job loss can also trigger panic attacks. Exam stress and fears like flying and heights can trigger an attack too.

There are no hard and fast answers as to why they occur, but traumatic or painful experiences and shock certainly play their part. When something happens to us, which is upsetting, it gets logged in the mind and if something similar happens again then the mind remembers the initial response and "feeds" it back to you. We cannot always make sense of why and when panic attacks occur but when they do, what is the best way of dealing with them?

Dizziness Tightness in chest
Tingling
Breathless **Trembling**
Sweating Numbness
PANIC ATTACK
Loss of control
Shivering Chest pain
Shaking Pounding heart
Feeling sick Choking
Closed Throat Hot Flushes

Try and identify the cause or the event that triggered the attacks and if and when you feel an attack coming on

- Deep breathing - breathe in deeply, counting to 4, pause, then breathe out counting to 4
- Stamp your feet - this will start to release the adrenaline
- Smell something strong like Olbas Oil which stimulates other senses

Jenna had failed her driving test 5 times! When she came to see me, I asked her if there was a pattern and she stated that each time she had failed, it had been at a roundabout where she had had a panic attack. No one had ever asked her about any memories she might have had relating to roundabouts. She told me about a bad accident she had been involved in – at a roundabout!

Although she was a passenger, every time she approached a roundabout when she was driving, her subconscious recalled the accident and the fear of it happening again triggered the stress response – or a panic attack. We quickly cleared the memory of the accident with EFT, plus how she felt about failing and the next time she took her test, she passed with no problems at roundabouts.

***

Jack (23) had recently been to a couple of celebrations where there were a lot of people. He felt hemmed in and had a full-blown panic attack which he believed was a heart attack and he convinced himself he was dying. On both occasions an ambulance was called but hospital test showed that there was nothing physically wrong with him.

His GP referred him to me in the belief that the cause was stress related. Jack was scared to go out in case it happened again. He could not remember any childhood experiences which may have triggered the panic attack. We started tapping and much to Jack's amazement, a memory came to him. He had been in a swimming pool aged nine and an older girl had clamped her legs around his head and pushed him under water! Guess what – he panicked and thought he was dying. Fortunately, he was rescued but when he was pulled out of the pool, there were lots of people around him and he felt hemmed in. His mind blocked most of this horrid experience but held on to the "hemmed in" part which triggered his panic attack years later. It's almost as if the subconscious is saying" I have been here before so I know what to do."

If you have panic attacks then rest assured you are not dying, but you do need to address the cause. Think back to when it first started and go through each memory associated with the attacks as you apply EFT.

See **Tapping Stuff**.

SOCIAL ANXIETY

Social anxiety can be described as extreme shyness which affects everyday activities and relationships. It destroys self-confidence, self - esteem, self-worth, and self-respect. It often starts in childhood and intensifies during adolescence, resulting in withdrawal and loneliness.

Most of us can identify with feeling a little anxious in new social situations, but someone with social anxiety worries excessively all the time.

In young children this anxiety can manifest itself in temper tantrums, "clingy" behaviour with parents, school refusal, crying, resisting participation in play or events at school.
It can be quite difficult for parents to identify social anxiety in their children if they are confident and chatty at home within the family where they feel safe.

OCD – Obsessive Compulsive Disorder

Distressing or frightening repetitive thoughts trigger responses or actions to try and make them go away. These thoughts seem to come into the mind automatically, even though logically or consciously you know that they are irrational. For example, continuous thoughts and fears about germs and diseases can prompt a hand washing ritual that is repetitive.

This may give short-term relief from the anxiety but then there is a need to do it again just to make sure!
Most OCD behaviours are linked to a fear or a need for perfection.

Common rituals include repeatedly:
• Checking light switches are off repeatedly
• Getting everything in place before eating, doing homework, going to bed
• Checking windows and doors repeatedly before leaving the house
• Cleaning phones and/or computers before each use
• Double checking sell-by dates on food labels
• Checking pockets/handbag before leaving house
• Worrying about harming others

OCD can be triggered by stress but is thought to be caused by childhood trauma or it may be genetic.

See **Tapping Stuff**
www.ocduk.org

MEMORY LOSS

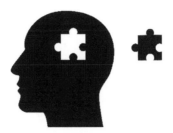

We all experience short term memory loss or "senior moments" at some time, regardless of age. Mislaid keys, forgotten "safe places" and not being able to find the right word or "brain freeze" are common to us all.

As stated previously, when the subconscious is on overload with stress, fear or any other emotion, the conscious mind struggles to operate efficiently. Does your mind go blank when you are nervous before or during an exam?

Memories provide crucial clues as to why and when certain conditions develop. Causes of memory loss include lack of sleep, some medications, an under active thyroid, grief, and depression.

Some medical conditions such as fibromyalgia can cause confusion and brain fog too.

Sometimes our memories are blocked – not to deceive us but to protect us. A traumatic event can be blocked until we are ready to deal with it, which may be never.

After a period, which could be months or years, the memory may be released. This can be due to a trigger of some sort which reactivates the memory or through a natural process when the subconscious determines that the person is ready to deal with it and heal.

When we are in a continuous state of trauma, like the hospital workers and carers during the pandemic, the mind ceases to absorb the horror. The body goes into automatic to be able to deal with the here and now, but there is a risk that the horrors will come back to haunt them and this needs to be managed and released.

I doubt that you can recall what you had for lunch three weeks ago, last Thursday – and why should you? It is not important so is not stored. Exam cramming has only one purpose and that is to store enough knowledge to pass the exam. Once done, it is usually forgotten quite quickly unless it is needed for practical or career purposes.

Like most of us, I can be a bit scatty sometimes, so I use several of the tips below, so I feel in control and calm.

When I was doing my master's degree in counselling psychology, I had a client who panicked whenever she felt "hemmed in". This meant she had to sit by the door at lectures, could not travel on the tube, struggled on the bus and in shops, pubs and at parties. She was understandably having a miserable time at uni. This was before I had discovered hypnosis and EFT (Emotional Freedom Technique – see Tapping Stuff).

We spent ages trying to work out why she felt like this and what had happened to cause it. At the end of term, I suggested that she sit down with her mum and go through old photos to see if that triggered any significant memories. It did! They found a photo of a fire engine and her mum recalled that when my client was two years old, she had managed to lock herself in the bathroom and her mum had to call the fire brigade to rescue her.

The subconscious mind had stored the memory and in order to protect her – gave her back the terror she felt in similar situations. Once we knew why she felt like this, and where it had come from, we had something to work with and she was soon in a much better place.

TIPS FOR MEMORY LOSS

- **Make** a weekly and daily timetable of tasks
- **Add** social events
- **Keep** to a regular and familiar routine
- **Write** important dates in your diary or Google calendar
- **Buy** a pill box if you are on medication to remind you what to take and when
- **Keep** your contacts up to date on your phone
- **Keep** keys and glasses in the same place
- **Make** notes at lectures and meetings
- **Use** highlighters for the important bits
- **Do** not spend too much time searching for misplaced items, avoid the stress, they will turn up!
- **Use** post-it notes to remind yourself of things you need to do or buy
- **When** you go out, put everything you need by the door in advance.
- **Stimulate** your memory by looking at photos

DEPRESSION

Some people use the word depression for having a bad day but in fact it's about *always* having bad days. Negative thoughts and feelings become a familiar pattern which seem to take over.

The monkey on the shoulder is in charge. Depression is labelled as mild, moderate, and severe, the latter often needing care as well as medication for the safety of the individual.

Sometimes depression has no apparent or obvious cause. However, in other cases, it may be caused by one or several factors, which include:

- **Genetics-** family history of depression
- **Biochemical -** the chemicals in the brain might be out of balance
- **A stressful event -** divorce, conflict, physical or sexual abuse, bullying, rape, death of a loved one, childhood trauma, relationship break-up
- **Personality**: - anxious, shy, perfectionist people and those who have low self-esteem.

Winston Churchill called his depression "the black dog" and said that it haunted him wherever he went. It has become a familiar phrase adopted by the World Health Organisation and MIND. You can find The Black Dog video on You Tube.

Symptoms generally include:

self harming   no point to anything
unworthy no joy guilty
nothing matters   no interests
sad   negative loss of appetite
suicidal fed up withdrawn
tearful lost   powerless
can't make decisions
DEPRESSION
insomnia worried all the time no motivation
useless   despondent
anxious inadequate
helpless   want to die   intolerant
lethargic irritable   lonely
everything is an effort

Do some reflection to determine when the depression started what may have triggered it. As I keep saying, everything starts somewhere.

Alice came to see me earlier this year with some specific personal issues which were cleared and when lockdown eased a bit, she came back stating she was depressed. She was tearful and felt overwhelmed with fear of going into a deep downward spiral. She had experienced her first panic attack at the weekend and convinced herself she was losing it.

As a result of lockdown, she had lost her job and had to postpone her wedding. She felt she had let everyone down, especially her fiancé. With some further exploration, her fear came from those around her who were on anti-

depressants - her future mother in law, and her own parents. She assumed that she would go the same way, and this terrified her.

Her future mother in law had suddenly changed from a happy go lucky lover of life to a depressive, following her own mothers' death. Alice then went on to tell me that her future mother in law had been abused and enslaved to her uncle as a young person with her own mothers blessing. Clearly there were unresolved issues there but rather than try and sort them out, anti-depressants were chosen.

Alice then told me about her dad who was self-harming and she was worried sick about him and also her mother who was not coping with her dad's depression. Both were on anti-depressants.

Her dad was a recently retired prison officer who had been attacked and badly hurt by an inmate. However, for various reasons the attack was covered up. There is a court case pending and Alice was recording her dad's experiences for evidence and she found this very upsetting.

As she was offloading and tapping for the emotions that were arising, she realised that she had absorbed a lot of "stuff" which was not hers and that she was not depressed after all.

Winter depression or SAD Seasonal Affective Disorder comes on in the Autumn and lifts in Spring.
The definitive cause of SAD is not fully understood but it is thought that contributory factors include our biological clocks being disrupted by lack of sunlight which causes a drop in Serotonin levels. (the" happy" hormone) and Melatonin levels which balance moods and sleep patterns.
www.nhs.uk/conditions/seasonal-affective-disorder-sad

ADHD, Autism and Asperger's

Conditions like **ADHD, Autism** and **Asperger's** tend to create more stress for those living with them, than for those diagnosed with the conditions. Each one is now recognised as a mental health condition as opposed to labelling people with bad behaviour, which used to be the case.

See **Tapping Stuff**
www.healthline.com/health/adhd
www.autism.org.uk/about/what-is/asd.aspx
www.autism.org.uk/about/what-is/asperger.aspx
www.aadduk.org

Dyslexia

Dyslexia is quite common and can cause a great deal of stress to the person who has it. It does not affect intelligence, but people with this condition often feel that they are perceived as thick or stupid. It can therefore lower confidence and self-esteem.

People with dyslexia usually read and write very slowly, and get words and letters muddled. They struggle with absorbing things written down and following sequences.

The first time I used EFT for dyslexia was with a young man of 16. He had other issues and when we had sorted these, he casually mentioned his dyslexia. He wrote down the words he could not spell (incorrectly) We tapped for each, one at a time and then he wrote it down again – this time correctly!

At the end of the school year, his dad sent me a copy of his school report which commented on the drastic improvement in his spelling!

See EFT for Dyslexia in **Tapping Stuff**
www.dyslexiaaction.org.uk
www.bdadyslexia.org.uk

Bipolar disorder

Bipolar disorder (traditionally known as manic depression) is characterised by extremes in mood, behaviour and thought patterns.

At one end of the scale is the mania which triggers impulsive behaviours and euphoria, energetic bursts and a lower need for sleep. At the other end of the scale is severe depression whereby staying in bed, exhaustion, self-loathing and hopelessness become the norm.

These cycles are unpredictable and can last for days, weeks or months. They damage relationships, academic progress and work performance and disrupt everyday life.
Bipolar disorder appears to be hereditary and tends to develop in adolescence and early adulthood. When diagnosed, this condition can be managed with medication.

Borderline Personality Disorders

This condition is also called Emotionally Unstable Personality Disorder which is easier to grasp. It is usually the result of childhood traumas, abuse, or neglect but there is also evidence of it being genetic as well. The symptoms may be mild or severe and usually manifest themselves during teenage years. It seems to be a "catch all" diagnosis and is associated with self-harm, anger and aggression, risk taking, binge eating or drinking, fear of abandonment and general emotional instability.

www.rethink.org/advice-and-information/about-mental-illness/learn-more-about-conditions/borderline-personality-disorder/

Psychosis

Psychosis means that the world is perceived differently from the norm. Psychosis sufferers experience, believe and see things from a different perspective. It is characterised by hallucinations and delusions.

Psychosis can be a one-off experience, but it is generally accepted as part of a long-term mental health condition. This includes Dementia, Alzheimer's or Parkinson's, disease. It can also be caused by a brain injury, a side effect of medication, an effect of drug abuse, or drug or alcohol withdrawal. (Cold Turkey)

Schizophrenia

There are numerous myths about schizophrenia which usually develop through lack of knowledge and understanding. This includes the belief that people who have this condition have split personalities.

It is fact a mental illness which affects the way you think, and the symptoms can affect everyday life and affects one in a hundred in the UK. It usually develops in early adulthood
• What to look for (not necessarily all at once):
• Hallucinations
• Delusions
• Disorganised thinking
• Lack of motivation
• Slow movement
• Changes in sleep patterns
• Lack of personal hygiene
• Changes in body language and emotions
• Limited interest in socialising
• Little or no sex drive

Only a psychiatrist can diagnose schizophrenia after a full psychiatric assessment. However, symptoms need to be present for at least a month before diagnosis can be made which can be incredibly stressful for all concerned. Just to complicate things further, there are seven different types of schizophrenia!

The causes are unknown but thought to be the result of several factors. Including brain chemistry, genetics and possibly birth complications. Some people develop the illness following a stressful event, such as the death of a loved one, loss of a job, moving to a new house or emigrating. There is also evidence to link the use of strong cannabis and the development of schizophrenia.

Unfortunately, there is not yet a cure for this condition and no clear pattern of recovery. Doctors prescribe anti-psychotic drugs to reduce and control symptoms.

www.rethink.org/advice-and-information/about-mental-illness/learn-more-about-conditions

4

PERSONAL STUFF

How well do you know yourself?

During my youth work years, one of the biggest challenges I had was to demonstrate the value of social education to the budget holders. Measuring personal growth and development is harder than demonstrating achievement through an examination pass. We did a lot of work with a retired Ofsted Inspector who developed a system that could be measured over time. He maintained that each of us needed Ten Personal and Social Skills to be well balanced individuals. Have a look at them and then identify areas that perhaps need a little work.

1. Self Esteem, self-awareness

- How do you describe yourself?
- How do others describe you?
- What is most important to you? e.g. beliefs? family? friends? possessions? achievement?
- How do you respond to different people? E.g. tutors, peers, police, parents?
- What are your strengths?
- In what ways do you need to improve?
- In what situations are you confident?
- In what situations do you lack confidence?
- Who has (or had) most influence on you?
- What are your ambitions?

2. Communication skills

- How well do you listen? Do others agree?
- Do you express yourself clearly?
- Do others always understand you?
- Are you happy contributing to group discussion?
- Are you aware of, and can you control, your body language?
- Can you discuss feelings easily?
- Are you confident contributing in all social situations?

3. Interpersonal skills
- Do you relate easily to those who differ by age,   gender, ethnicity or socially?
- Which age groups do you prefer to be with?
- Do you form friendships easily?
- Do you enjoy working with others?
- Do you take the lead in a group?
- Can you motivate others to work with you?
- Are you happy to support others' efforts and accept their leadership?
- Are you tolerant of others' differences and mistakes?
- Are you sensitive to others' needs?
- Do you encourage others to learn and improve?

4. Explore and manage feelings
- Are you aware of how you feel each day?
- How do your feelings affect your actions?
- How aware are you of changes of mood and what influences them?
- What makes you happy?
- What makes you angry?
- Do you ever act impulsively, without thinking?
- Do you ever regret acting impulsively, because of the consequences?
- When are you frightened?
- Do you behave differently when frightened?
- How do you manage your feelings, and your actions?

5. Understand and identify with others
- Do you stereotype people different from you? (e.g. by gender, race, religion)
- Are you stereotyped by others? How do you feel about that?
- How do you feel about those who differ from you, e.g. by disability, homeless?
- Can you empathise with them?
- Have you had anything stolen or suffered violence? If so, how did you feel?
- How do you think victims of robbery and violence feel?

- Do you want to help those who suffer discrimination? How?
- How can you think of others as people rather than impersonal stereotypes?
- When you empathise with someone, how does that affect your behaviour?
- When you empathise with someone, does that alter their reactions to you?

6. Values development

- How do you like others to behave towards you? With respect, consideration?
- What is honesty? Why is it important? What happens without it?
- How do you feel when something you value is destroyed?
- Why do you value some things rather than others?
- Why do you respect some people more than others?
- Do you recognise spiritual values? If so, could you describe them if asked?
- Do you respect others' beliefs? Do you know what they are?
- Can you list the values you would like to live your life by? (See Values in **Mind Stuff**)
- Is anything stopping you from doing so?

7. Problem solving

- Do you rush at problems, think about them, or hope they will go away?
- Is it helpful to share problems with others? Are two heads better than one?
- Who do you turn to for help? Friends, parents, others?
- Do you define the problem, assemble information and explore alternatives?
- Problems may have several underlying causes; can you solve them all?
- Where do you obtain information and support?
- Is it easier to "solve" other people's problems than your own? Why?

- Does writing a problem and possible solutions down help you to be objective?
- How can you learn from others' experiences, successes, and failures?
- Can problems be opportunities for growth, i.e.be beneficial? Examples?

8. Negotiation skills

- When you are working with others, how are decisions reached?
- Do you try to impose your views? Does this always work? If not, why not?
- Do you listen to others' views? Why is this important?
- How do you reach mutually acceptable solutions?
- Can everyone always win? Or do you have to accept compromise?
- Do you sometimes prefer confrontation to compromise? Does this work?
- When you do reach agreement in a group, do you find this satisfying?
- Are you happy to let someone else represent your views? Is trust easy?
- Are group decisions usually better than individual ones? if so, why?
- Are you able to learn from negotiation? i.e. benefit from others' experience?
- When working in a group, do you discover others' feelings and concerns?
- Do you ensure all group members share the same expectations?
- Do you reflect on your successes to ensure you can repeat them?
- Do you consciously build on your strengths and work on weaknesses?

9. Action Planning

- Do you feel in control of your whole life? If not, which areas do you control?

- Do you act impulsively, or do you always consider the consequences first?
- Do you regret any impulsive actions? What would you do differently now?
- Do you set short- and long-term goals? Should you? Such as?
- How do you know what is possible? e.g.: accommodation, training, a job?
- Do you know your strengths and weaknesses, i.e.: what you are capable of?
- Do you prepare action plans and think about how to implement them?
- If others are affected, do you involve them fully in the planning?
- Are you patient enough to wait for the right opportunity to implement plans?
- What must you do to take more control of your life?

10. Reviewing Skills
- Do you learn from your mistakes and try not to repeat them?
- Do you celebrate success and achievement?
- Do you consciously build on your strengths and work on weaknesses?
- Do you regularly review progress, so you can act if necessary?
- Do you discuss your personal plans and progress with friends? And theirs?
- Do you benefit fully from each other's experience?
- Do you record your achievements so that others can credit you with them?
- When working in a group, do you check out others' feelings and concerns?
- Do you ensure all group members are clear about expectations?
- Do you use reviewing to control your learning and where you are going?
- Does reviewing and reflecting on the past help you to plan the future?

Adapted from Quality Work with Young People by John Huskins 1994 (with permission)

"Be yourself because everyone else is already taken"
Oscar Wilde

SELF ESTEEM

"*Self-esteem is how we value and perceive ourselves. It's based on our opinions and beliefs about ourselves, which can sometimes feel really difficult to change."* **MIND**

Self-esteem and emotional health are closely related and is essential to make positive lasting relationships. Self-esteem embraces self-respect, self-worth and self-reliance.

It is usually described in three ways: Inflated Self-esteem, High Self-esteem, and Low Self-esteem

Inflated Self-esteem - these think that they are better than anyone else, they are competitive and measure life through perceived success and achievement. They do not like any criticism, constructive or otherwise and find it hard to listen to advice. They do not learn from their mistakes, avoid responsibility, and blame others, rather than appreciating them.

High Self-esteem - these believe and trust in their ability to deal with whatever life throws at them. They feel safe and secure within their own skins and when they are off balance, they can bounce back. They are not seen as arrogant by others but self-assured and in control.

Low Self-esteem - These people don't value or trust themselves, feel insecure, unhappy and fear failure. When they do feel good about their lives, the slightest blip can knock them back. They are easily influenced, feel inadequate, unimportant, unloved and are full of doubts.

I see many clients with low self-esteem, and it can destroy so many aspects of life which are resolvable.

BONUS OFFER
Download my Self Esteem audio on
www.stressworxbooks.com

"You wouldn't worry so much about what others think of you if you realised how seldom they do".
Eleanor Roosevelt

BODY IMAGE
A negative body image can cause stress and low self-esteem as well as feelings of inferiority and shame together with a lack of body confidence.

What do you think and feel when you see your body image in a mirror or photo? Are you comfortable with it? Do you accept that you may not be perfect, or do you worry about being too fat, too thin, too tall, or too short? Do you accept yourself or worry about trying to change to feel better?

Body Confidence was the theme for Mental Health Awareness in May 2019 who carried out a survey with You Gov. Over 5,000 people (with 13 being the youngest) were involved and it found that an alarming number of people were either ashamed, disgusted, anxious, depressed and even suicidal about their body images.

"You have been criticising yourself for years and it hasn't worked. Try approving of yourself and see what happens"
Louise Hay

Extreme dislike is described as Body Dysmorphia which is a recognised mental health condition.

www.bddfoundation.org/helping-you/questionnaires-do-i-have-bdd

I saw a lovely post on FB recently called "The Seven Wonders of the World" - To See, To Hear, To Taste, To Smell, To Touch, To Move and to Love How often do we really appreciate them?

TIPS FOR A POSITIVE BODY IMAGE

- **Eat** *healthily and stay active*

- **Treat** *your body with respect*

- **Look** *after your skin*

- **Wear** *clothes that you feel good in.*

- **Focus** *on the parts of your body that you DO like*

- **List** *the things you like about yourself and read out loud every day*

- **Try** *not to be influenced by the media.*

- **Spend** *time with people who don't judge you but accept you for who you are*

- **Don't** *assume that those with "perfect "bodies are happier than you!*

- **Do** *something useful to help someone in need*

- **Don't** *compare yourself to others*

- **Accept** *that you don't need to be perfect*

- **Pamper** *yourself regularly*

- **Be grateful** *for what your body can do – breathing. movement, your senses and so on*

Here is a recipe to improve your perception of yourself – Some things may be glaringly obvious to you but maybe not all.

SELF CONFIDENCE

Confidence and self-esteem are not quite the same although they are obviously linked. Confidence describes how we feel about our ability to perform roles, functions and tasks. Self-esteem describes how we feel about ourselves, the way we look, the way we think and whether we feel worthy and valued.

People with low self-esteem often have low confidence too but it is possible for those with high self-esteem to lack confidence. Likewise, those with low self-esteem can be confident carrying out certain tasks.

A simple definition of self-confidence is having faith in yourself.
As with most things, self-confidence tends to be the product of our upbringing and how we see ourselves.

The degree of confidence that we feel can change depending on the situation. Familiar and comfortable tasks trigger more confidence and control than new challenges which may take us out of our comfort zone.

Lack of confidence can be caused by:
• Fear of the unknown

- Criticism
- Feeling unprepared
- Poor time management
- Lack of knowledge
- Previous failures
- Misinformation
- Worry about what others think
- Ridicule or humiliation
- Bullying

All sorts of things can knock our confidence, a snide remark, or upsetting experience. Maybe you had an embarrassing job interview or a crunch in your car which made you hesitant next time around. Blame your subconscious and get tapping!

See **Tapping Stuff** for confidence and have a go at implementing the tips on the next page.

There is a fine line between over confidence and arrogance. Most of us respect confident people (and may even envy them) but are likely to avoid arrogant people with huge egos who believe they are better than anyone else.

Ask your partner, friends, family, and colleagues to tell you three things they like about you – Its good for the ego!

"Everybody is a genius. But if you judge a fish by its ability to climb a tree, it will live its whole life believing that it is stupid."
Albert Einstein

RELATIONSHIPS

"Don't chase people. Be yourself, do your own thing and work hard. The right people – the ones who really belong in your life – will come to you. And stay."
Will Smith

All relationships are unique, some lasting for a lifetime, some for many years, and others are short-term as people come and go within our lives.
Family relationships are the first ones we experience, and if our early years are happy, stable, safe and secure with lots of love, affection and trust, then this will become our expectation for the future.

If, however, childhood years are insecure, with feelings of being unloved, unwanted, or unneeded, this could probably hinder faith in others, as well as our ability to make strong, lasting relationships.

To initiate, develop and maintain relationships we all need to be able to communicate, and have patience, tolerance, and a shared understanding of what is important to us. People we care about are accepted for who they are, and we expect them in return to accept all our strengths and weaknesses as well.

Most family relationships are tested at some point, and whilst this is to be expected, they can cause stress and upsets.

The pandemic certainly tested us all, bringing a lot of sudden and new changes to all our lives. Parents were trying to balance work, childcare, home schooling and self-care whilst dealing with unfamiliar situations. Tensions, conflict, arguments, and bickering tended to escalate more quickly than normal, adding to the stress. As you know, students were sent home early, holiday jobs became hard to come by and uncertainty took over.

Compromise is the key to harmonious family life, but this can be difficult when attitudes, beliefs and values differ, adding to uncertainty about the future. Having family meals or a specified family time where feelings are shared, and news discussed is a useful exercise to keep dialogues open and reduce tension through clear communication.

"Friends are the family we choose for ourselves" applies to student life. It's important to have a few people in your life that you can share your feelings and thought with. Sometimes, in residential halls and student houses, some people become excluded. This may be from their own choosing, but isolation can lead to severe depression and worse so do keep an eye out for the loners. Kindness doesn't hurt anyone!

"Unexpected kindness is the most powerful, least costly and most underrated agent of human change"
Bob Kerrey

CONFIDENCE TIPS

- **Dress to impress** – *if you look good, you will feel good*

- **Create your own style** – *wear what makes you feel good regardless of fashion trends*

- **Stand tall**

- **When in doubt** – *leave it out! Trust your instincts and surround yourself with positive people.*

- **Identify** *your strengths and be proud of them*

- **Don't** *put yourself down by comparing yourself to others*

- **Set** *achievable goals for yourself and celebrate success*

- **Try** *big picture thinking and put things in perspective*

- **Be** *true to yourself*

- **Organise** *your room, clothes / desk / work so you can find things easily without stressing*

- **Plan and prepare** – *think ahead and have a Plan B*

- **Be kind**, *polite and respectful to others, they will notice*

- **Smile**

- **Believe** *in yourself*

- **Focus** *on solutions not problems*

- **Learn** *from mistakes and move on*

- **Take control** *of your monkey, that inner voice*

- **Make decisions** *that are right for you by weighing up the pros and cons*

- **Be assertive** *not arrogant*

- **Visualise** *new situations until they become your reality*

EXPECTATIONS

The most important relationship we ever have, at any age, is with ourselves. If we try to comply with the expectations and beliefs of others all the time, then life can be challenging. Some would say "anything for an easy life" but will life be easy if you cannot live with yourself comfortably? Expectations or pressure can challenge or motivate us to do our best. However, unrealistic expectations are not helpful, and can have a negative impact on our thoughts, feelings, and behaviour, causing undue stress. Relationships can suffer due to external or unrealistic expectations.

We may have been expected to follow cultural or racial beliefs and traditions, even though we may not have agreed with them. (Examples are FGM, arranged marriage, sex before marriage, abortion.)

Parents, teachers and tutors may have expected high grades and academic success, or we may have felt pressure from sports teammates or trainer to participate and do well regardless of whatever else was going on in our lives.

Society also has expectations, and through media and advertising, there is pressure to behave in certain ways or buy certain products.

What about the expectations of your university? What about your own expectations of yourself? Are they too high or too low?

We all want to be thought well of and meeting the perceived expectations of others is one way of doing that. However, beware being taken advantage of! Continuously trying not to let anyone down can be stressful and the only person you let down in the end is yourself. Finding that work life balance, managing time and saying no on occasion is worth considering.

Maria was 14 and a great rower. She was good and loved her chosen sport. She was so good that she was moved up from the junior team to the seniors where most of the girls were over eighteen. She was terrified of letting them down and believed that they had high expectations of her to win at every race. If they didn't win, she believed it was her fault. She started to have dizzy spells and passed out when her team lost. She tapped for her fears and expectations and recalled a memory from age 9 when the coach shouted at her and blamed her when her team lost. She was devastated but it was this memory that was triggering the problem at 14. It was soon cleared, and Maria's confidence and self-belief returned.

LOVE

Love is probably the most used and misused word in the English language and one of the most powerful emotions that we can experience. We all love in different ways – pets, families, friends, all by degree. We all know that love that is not returned can be incredibly painful and stressful, but positive experiences of love "make the world go around." Love is the main subject of poems, songs, films, and books, but what is it?

When we are falling in love, we want to be with our partner all the time, and when we're not together, we're thinking and yearning to be back together because we need that person and feel empty and incomplete without our loved one.

Unconditional love has no limits or conditions attached. It's when we trust the other with our life and when we would do anything for each other. Being in love with someone makes us put our partner's needs and happiness before our own. You have no secrets from each other and accept any weaknesses or faults.

Love, when it is returned and equal, can make your world a better place. You feel understood, safe, and valued.

In the traditional order of life events, when we are in love, we want to settle down and be with that person all the time. Some opt for marriage or civil partnerships; others prefer to live together without the celebration (and stress) of a ceremony and celebration.

Student life provides more opportunity than at any other time to explore living with others, either as a partner or as a friend.

Living together helps to explore and consolidate values – which behaviours you can live and which you can't!

REJECTION

As we know, not all relationships work out the way we want or expect them to, and most of us have probably experienced "being dumped" at some time in our lives. We possibly also did some "dumping" too. If you are on the receiving end, it can be very painful indeed, and if you had low self-esteem or lacked self-confidence, you may have felt inadequate.

Not so! It just wasn't meant to be. Hopefully, we learn from these experiences and move on.

Obviously, breaking up is easier up when the relationship is not serious. However, if you really did care and were not expecting rejection, it came as a shock. Common reactions include feeling stunned and unable to find the right words to respond. This stress response may have made you feel shaky, dizzy, and sick, wanting to cry or run away. Your heart may have pounded, and you couldn't think straight.

Over the following few days, whenever you thought about what happened, you may have felt hurt and angry, finding it hard to eat, sleep or concentrate on anything. You may have wanted to be left alone to ask yourself what went wrong and dwell on the misery you felt. All perfectly normal and shows how resilient we are. With any form of loss, time is a great healer and tapping can help the process.

See **Tapping Stuff.**

SEXUALITY

"Human sexuality is the way people experience and express themselves sexually. This involves biological, erotic, physical, emotional, social, or spiritual feelings" Wikipedia

Sexuality is personal to all of us, but our society has a tendency to label people. However, many people do not actually understand the different terminology.

Straight / Heterosexual - Attracted to people of the opposite sex or gender.

LGBTQI + is the politically correct collective term given to the following: -

Lesbian - females who are attracted to people of the same sex or gender

Gay / Homosexual - males who are attracted to people of the same sex or gender

Bisexual - Attracted to both men and women.
Transgender - A person whose sense of gender identity is different from the sex they were born with. Sexual orientation varies and is not dependent on gender identity.

Questioning - someone who is unsure of their gender identity or sexual orientation.

Intersex - Is a general term used for a variety of conditions in which a person is born with a reproductive or sexual anatomy that doesn't fit the typical definitions of female or male.

The + covers
Pansexual - Attracted to romantic and sexual partners of any gender, sex or sexual identity

Asexual - Not sexually attracted to anyone.
Some people also choose the labels **'queer'** or **'fluid' to describe** themselves as a way of expressing their own personal feelings.

Being comfortable with our own sexuality is crucial for our mental and emotional health and wellbeing.

During teenage years, it can be confusing and there is an assumption that everyone is "straight" unless they "come out". This seems to very unfair – being expected to make a statement or declaration about something so personal.

Sadly, many parents lack observation skills where their pubescent or teenage children are concerned and may not notice the stress, tension, or changes in behaviour. Finding the courage to tell friends, parents, and extended families that you are not "straight" can be very daunting.

Sexuality and Mental Health

Statistics show that LGBTI people have an increased risk of depression, anxiety, substance abuse, homelessness, self-harming and suicidal thoughts, compared with the general population. This particularly affects young LGBTI people who are coming to terms with their sexuality and may be experiencing victimisation and bullying.

Examples of the stressful experiences that can affect the mental health of an LGBTI person are:
*   Feeling different from other people
*   Being bullied (verbally or physically)
*   Feeling pressure to deny or change their sexuality
*   Feeling worried about coming out
*   Fear of being rejected or isolated
*   Feeling unsupported or misunderstood.

You can find the timeline of LGBT history on Wikipedia – it is a fascinating read which starts in Roman times.

LONELINESS

Loneliness is a painful emotion which most of us can identify with. We can even feel lonely when we have other people around us, but hopefully that is short lived. However, the impact of long-term loneliness on mental health can be quite serious.

Being lonely is one of the greatest human fears, and it can be incredibly stressful and debilitating. Many old people become very depressed when they are alone for long periods of time especially when many of their friends have already died. Unlike the elderly, who may have mobility problems, younger people can get out and about. We all need human interaction, a kind word, or a hug, to keep us feeling valued and needed.

In "normal times" it was possible to avoid being alone by joining clubs and societies but during the pandemic loneliness took on a new meaning. Being forced to stay at home for those living alone was especially hard.
The Mental Health Foundation conducted a survey of 2,221 UK adults at the beginning of April 2020 to find out how the outbreak was affecting people's wellbeing. It asked participants to reflect on the previous two weeks.

Almost a quarter of adults living under the coronavirus lockdown in the UK said they felt lonely, with the most affected group found to be young people aged 18 to 24 with 44 per cent admitting to experiencing loneliness. Is this something you are familiar with?

If we are proactive, reach out and invite people to go somewhere with us, it's better than waiting to be asked. Others will not know we are lonely unless we tell them.

COMMUNICATION
Many if not most relationships that breakdown, do so due to a lack of communication. We are all guilty of making

assumptions or not stating what seems obvious to us but may not be to others.

Communication is key to all relationships and research from Professor Albert Mehrabian claims that words are only 7% of what we are trying to convey. The tone of our voices is 38% but body language accounts for 55%! The percentages have been challenged but tone and body language are certainly as important as the words themselves.

As a therapist, I look carefully at body language of my clients speaks volumes.

How often have you thought that the messages you receive via text or email are abrupt or insensitive because you could not see the person's body language?

No wonder we get mixed messages via social media!

Facial expressions, gestures, eye contact, posture, and tone of voice speak louder than words. Silence also speaks volumes! The way we listen, look, move, and react tells the other person whether we care, if we are being truthful, and how well we're listening.

Within our multi-cultural society, we need to be aware that eye contact in Western Europe and the US shows interest and attention to what is being said.

However, in some cultures, including Hispanic, Asian, Middle Eastern and Native American, eye contact is considered to be disrespectful or rude. Women may especially avoid eye contact with men because it can be misinterpreted as a sign of sexual interest.

The tone of our voice is also especially important (38%) and can easily be misconstrued and cause stress to the person on the receiving end.

Aggressive communication is using a forceful or hostile manner, and usually involves allocating blame or calling people names. Aggressive voice tone together with body language projects unfriendliness and often means trouble!

Passive communication is not expressing our thoughts or feelings or asking for what we want. Passive communication results in feeling like we don't matter because we don't stand up for ourselves. Eventually this affects our self-esteem and possibly makes us feel resentful for not being heard.

Assertive communication involves clearly expressing what we think, how we feel and what we want, without demanding that we have things our way. Assertive communication increases the likelihood of achieving what we want, avoiding conflict and maintaining good relationships.

Touch is, of course, also an important part of communication and a big hug speaks volumes! It is however also open to cultural interpretation. A handshake is the traditional greeting in the UK and US, but in many European countries, a kiss on both cheeks is the norm, or a high five or fist bump is a popular casual greeting. (Virtual hugs and elbow bumping are just not the same!) In many cultures the left hand is for toilet use but scouts worldwide use a left handshake – confusing!

Inappropriate touch is something that most of us instinctively know is wrong as we feel uncomfortable and feel the need to check out why it is happening.

We all know that if anyone touches us in any way that makes us feel insecure, uncomfortable, or afraid, we should tell someone. It may be perfectly innocent, but it may not!

Julie was fifteen when she realised that her teacher was being overly familiar with her, and flirting. She was flattered but in retrospect recognised that her response was due to her need for love and affection. Her dad had left her mum the previous year after being caught out in an affair and it was Julie who told her mum.

She felt guilty about the family break-up and missed her dad. She fell in love with the teacher and did not think they were doing anything wrong having underage sex. The relationship dwindled when she left school and she kept it a secret and only told her closest friend. In her early twenties, she realised that he had "groomed her" and she needed to deal with her mixed emotions. She had lost touch with her friend and was unaware that she had married a policeman and during all the Jimmy Saville revelations, she had told her husband about Julie. The next thing that Julie knew, the police were on her doorstep! After a great deal of soul-searching, she revealed the teacher's name and discovered to her horror that she had not been the only young woman that the teacher had seduced! He lost his job and was prosecuted.

Of course, this can work both ways. I have had a few clients who have had allegations made against them for inappropriate behaviour with young people. They were false allegations made by people who had an axe to grind.

The effect on the accused adults was devastating, with investigations, suspicion and mistrust developing in their workplace.

If allegations are found to be true then the perpetrators deserve everything they get, but false accusations can be soul destroying.

Listening

Listening is obviously an important part of communicating with others. We adopt different listening styles in different situations. Think about the way you listen to a friend who is upset as opposed to being in the pub, or in a lecture

Levels of Listening......

* _Ignoring_
* _Pretend listening_
* _Selective Listening – hearing only what interests us_
* _Active Listening – Paying attention_
* _Empathic Listening – identifying with what is being said to us_

Telephone listening

Telephone listening is obviously different from face to face conversation in that you do not have eye contact or body language to help identify what is NOT being said.

It is therefore harder to assess the emotions of the person on the other end of the line (especially with people you don't know).

This makes active and attentive listening more important than within a face to face conversation.

Most universities have counselling services, and some have telephone helplines too. Whilst they have their place, there is no substitute for face to face communication. During lockdowns, most of us learned how to use Zoom and similar apps, which enable visual contact as well as listening.

Confidentiality

If you are listening to a friend who is telling you something private and personal, s/he would not expect you to then tell everyone you know or post on social media.

This works both ways, so it is always advisable to have an agreement between you. The rule of thumb is to keep a confidence unless someone's life is considered to be at risk.

Questions

Questions help to clarify what is being said and confirm that the listener is interested in what is being said!

There are closed questions which just require a yes or no answer, and open questions which usually start with "how, what, when, why, who and where."

We can expect a better response from an open question. When working or living with people who are obviously struggling, gentle open questions are always best to find out what is causing them stress and anxiety.

A friend in need is a friend indeed. Making time to sit and chat with those close to us, can help problems come into proportion and offloading or venting feelings can stop them building up into something bigger. There is another age old saying that a problem shared is a problem halved. This may not be accurate, but problems seem smaller and less overwhelming when shared and another perspective can help with finding solutions,

Silent and **Listen** have the same letters!

If someone is troubled and comes to you, they may feel apprehensive, but they have obviously chosen you for a reason! When we know, like and trust another person, it is easier to share problems. Whatever doubts you may have about being able to help – listening and being heard goes a long way.

Helpful responses:
* *That must have been difficult*
* *You don't deserve that*
* *How does that make you feel?*
* *What do you think you can do about it?*
* *Can I just clarify …*
* *As I understand it …*
* *What do you think your options might be?*
* *Is there anything else you need to say?*
* *Its ok to cry*
* *Thank you for sharing with me*
* *This must be really hard for you*

- *Am I right in thinking that …*
- *Tell me again about …*

The following tips are from a Listening Skills programme I delivered for volunteers in my village who wanted to be "listeners" for those who were isolated and lonely within the community. You may find them useful.

LISTENING GUIDELINES (face to face)

- **Find** *a quiet space without any distractions*

- **Ensure** *that you both feel relaxed with each other*

- **Speak** *in a calm voice*

- **Try not** *to interrupt*

- **Allow** *them time and space to think*

- **Believe** *what they say to you*

- **Accept** *that the situation is very real to them*

- **Try** *not to give advice nor make comparisons*

- **Empathise** - *imagine being in their shoes*

- **Watch** *for nonverbal clues to understand feelings*

- **Try** *not to react to what they are telling you*

- **Avoid** *sarcasm*

- **Do** *not make assumptions – check!*

- **Ask** *open questions where appropriate*

- **Don't** *try to have the last word*

- **Keep** *an open mind*

- **If** *things get heated or emotional, take a break*

- **Stay** *in the present -avoid wondering what is coming next*

LISTENING GUIDELINES (face to face)

(Continued)

- **Listen** *to what is not being said, be aware of tension or hesitation*

- **Keep** *eye contact with the person throughout*

- **Summarise** *at appropriate points*

- **Help** *them to explore options to move forward*

- **Do not** *offer advice*

- **Decide** *on action points together*

- **Arrange** *to meet again if appropriate*

The Written Word

Long gone are the days of letter writing by hand, where letters could be kept and re-read again and again. Technology has taken over, and typing is undoubtedly faster than writing with a fountain pen but shortened text language, can often lead to wrong or misleading messages. We must not lose sight of the fact that correct grammar and spelling are needed for exams and job applications.

PERFECTIONISM
"Perfectionism is self – abuse of the highest order"
Anne Wilson Schaaf

The word perfect makes us think of positive things but what is perfection? Is it a perception or an illusion? Doing your best in achieving goals is admirable, providing you are not too disappointed if you do not do as well as you thought you had or hoped to do.

However, feeling being driven to be perfect all the time can become obsessive, unhealthy, and unachievable. The result is fear of failure, feeling inadequate, guilt, low self-esteem, lack of self - respect. distress, insomnia, depression, troubled relationships, reduced productivity, and dissatisfaction with life. Have a look through the tips and see which ones may be useful for you.

Distressed when goals not met

Unrealistic goals Defensiveness

Low self esteem Dread of Failure

Fear of mistakes

Rejection   Overly critical of self

PERFECTIONISM

Unrealistic standards

High expectations of self

Procrastination All or nothing thinking

Ensures completion Unable to accept criticism

Choosing safe tasks

Driven to be the best never satisfied

Hiding mistakes from others

Focus on results

Avoidance of risk

TIPS FOR PERFECTIONISM

- **Stop** *listening to the monkey on your shoulder*

- **Check** - *are your thoughts factual or your interpretation of events?*

- **Stop** *jumping to negative conclusions without evidence*

- **Ask** *yourself is the situation as bad as you think?*

- **Check** - *is the worst-case scenario likely to happen?*

- **Check** - *will this matter in 2, 3, or 5 years' time?*

- **Be kind** *to yourself*

- **Set** *small goals, record, and celebrate each achievement*

- **Try** *and remove "should" from your vocabulary*

- **Stop** *comparing yourself to others*

- **Accept** *that self-doubt is normal*

- **Learn** *from mistakes rather than dwell on them*

- **Tell** *yourself that you* **are** *good enough every day*

FINANCIAL STRESS
"Money, money, money, it's a rich man's world "
Abba, 1976

Not having enough money can be incredibly stressful and is familiar to most students. Continuous worry about trying to make ends meet can put tremendous strain on relationships and student life.

We know that post pandemic Britain will see mega job losses and debt increases. Materialism, envy, greed, comparison to others, and spending money we do not really have may not be possible anymore. Our culture tends to measure success by monetary value, rather than achievement or happiness. Time for a culture shift!

Scams too, can cause stress as well as humiliation and shame for being conned. The temptation to gamble is not worth considering but many students do!
Rather than wasting energy on worrying and stressing about money, count your blessings. Think about your loved ones and your health, both worth their weight in gold or beyond price.

MONEY STRESS TIPS

- **Use** *credit cards carefully*
- **Try** *and pay them off monthly*
- **Work** *out a monthly budget*
- **Don't** *spend what you haven't got!*
- **Keep** *a note of expenditure*
- **Don't** *exceed your overdraft*
- **Determine** *between needs and wants*
- **Take** *advantage of student discounts*
- **Shop** *around for bargains*
- **Reduce** *your takeaway meals*
- **Consider** *SIM card only for your phone*
- **Make** *a packed lunch if you can instead of spending at the sandwich shop or cafeteria*
- **Make** *do with clothes and shoes instead of buying new or go to Charity shops*
- **Visit** *your local Citizens Advice Bureau for advice*
- **Set** *up an emergency fund*
- **Find** *part time work for the holidays*
- **Check out** *the money saving website*

5

HEALTH

STUFF

"A calm mind brings inner strength and self-confidence, so that's very important for good health."
Dalai Lama

When we are children, unless we are around sick people, we tend to take our health for granted. As students, this is also true but Covid-19 has shown us all that we are not infallible, and our health is precious.

Looking after ourselves - mentally, emotionally as well as physically, can help reduce stress on both body and mind.
As stated in **Mind Stuff**, the connection between our minds and bodies is powerful and understated or misunderstood. Whatever is causing you stress, it will inevitably cause physical health issues.

The reverse is also true. Health problems affect our stress levels as well as our mental health and wellbeing.

When our brain experiences high degrees of stress, our bodies react accordingly. The immune system weakens, making us vulnerable to illness, colds, aches and pains.

Chronic (ongoing) stress can have a serious impact on our physical health as well. If we experience   continuous chronic stress   our bodies are on high alert all the time causing the   autonomic nervous system to be overactive, which is likely to damage the   body. When our brain experiences high degrees of stress, our bodies react accordingly. The immune system weakens, making us vulnerable to illness, colds, aches and pains.

Chronic (ongoing) stress can have a serious impact on our physical health as well. If we experience   continuous chronic stress   our bodies are on high alert all the time causing the   autonomic nervous system to be overactive, which is likely to damage the body and make us vulnerable to viral infections and illness.

The automatic nervous system is responsible for-
- Digestion
- Blood pressure
- Heart rate
- Urination and defecation
- Pupillary response
- Breathing rate
- Sexual responses
- Body temperature
- Metabolism
- Electrolyte balance
- Production of body fluids including sweat and saliva
- Emotional responses

Early symptoms may be mild, like headaches and increased susceptibility to colds and stomach upsets but as stress levels continue more serious health problems may develop. They include, but are not limited to:
- Diabetes
- Hair loss
- Heart disease/angina
- Heart attacks
- Strokes
- Sleep problems
- Muscle tension
- Overactive thyroid
- Weight gain
- Sexual dysfunction
- Tooth and gum disease
- Ulcers

SLEEP

Are you a night owl? One of the best ways to ensure that we stay as healthy as possible is to get enough sleep. It is sleep that allows our bodies to relax, refresh, repair and renew, ready for the next day. We feel more alert, more energetic, happier, and better able to function following a good night's sleep. Think of sleep being rather like recharging your phone so it can work properly.

Without sleep, we suffer and find it hard to cope with whatever is going on around us. Lack of adequate sleep also weakens the immune system, making us more vulnerable to illness.

Insomnia is difficulty in getting to sleep, waking during the night and not being able to get back to sleep and just not getting enough - making us feel drained and not able to cope during the day. This in turn makes us feel stressed, and the cycle continues as we become more stressed, tense and edgy, worrying about whether we will sleep or not.

Lack of sleep is caused by a range of things – physical pain and discomfort, fear, anxiety, painful memories which "haunt us at night, depression worry or stress. Insomnia can also be caused by an addiction to medications, caffeine, nicotine, alcohol, or other heavier drugs.

Acute insomnia is suffering from sleep problems for few weeks. Suffering for an even longer period it is called *chronic* insomnia.

What to look for:
- Having difficulties falling asleep
- Waking up several times each night and having problems falling asleep again
- Feeling drowsy when waking up
- Depending on alcohol or medication to be able to fall asleep
- Feeling tired during the day
- Feeling irritable and uncoordinated
- Having problems with concentration or memory
- Increased risk of accidents
- Experiencing "restless legs syndrome" (painful, tingling feeling in your legs)

Reduced concentration
Stomach problems
Obesity   Memory loss
accident prone   grumpy
LACK of SLEEP
Risk of infections
Weakened immune system
Forgetful   raised blood pressure
Heart disease
Early aging   Diabetes
Skin problems   irritable

Negative effects of too little sleep
Not getting enough sleep can have severe negative effects on health, so if you are suffering from insomnia it is crucial that you get help as soon as possible. Here are some effects.

Some people struggle to sleep because they are worried about waking at a certain time. Because I don't hear alarms, I use another method to wake up. It sounds totally wacky, but it has never let me down! This is nothing to do with EFT but tap on the middle of your forehead for the time you want to wake, i.e. six taps for 6.00. Tap firmly and then for half an hour, a gentle tap will do. Try it!

When you are ready to sleep:

• **Deep breathing.** *Close your eyes and take deep slow breaths as your body relaxes.*

• **Progressive muscle relaxation.** *Starting at your toes, tense all the muscles as tightly as you can, then relax them. Work your way up your body, feet, legs, thighs, hips, stomach, chest, arms, shoulders, neck and head.*

• **Count -** *backwards from 100 on each outward breath*

• **Visualise or pretend** *that you are in a special, peaceful place where you feel calm and relaxed.*

• **Imagine** *writing down all the things keeping you awake on a wall, graffiti style, then painting over it with thick black paint until all the words have gone.*

SLEEP TIGHT!

SLEEP TIPS

Most of us have difficulty sleeping on occasion but stress is a major factor in keeping you awake – tense muscles, worry and anxiety are not the best way to get a good night's sleep.

- **Have** *a regular bedtime and establish a routine*

- **Soak** *in a warm bath before bed*

- **Have** *a warm drink but not caffeine*

- **Read** *a book or magazine*

- **Turn** *off all devices*

- **Set** *your alarm to wake up at the same time each day*

- **Have** *a nap during the day to catch up on lost sleep but limit it to thirty minutes*

- **Avoid** *eating late*

- **Monitor** *your caffeine intake after 4pm. Try and cut it out for a few days and see if it makes a difference.*

- **Wear** *comfortable nightwear*

- **Make** *sure you are warm enough.*

- **Check** *that the mattress is firm for support*

- **Buy** *a pillow that suits you*

- **Keep** *your bedroom well ventilated*

- **Avoid** *loud noise*

- **Keep** *a journal to offload your thoughts from the day*

Health Anxiety

As soon as you get an ache or pain do you Google it and then imagine the worst-case scenario?! Do people around you accuse you of being a hypochondriac or overreacting to your perceived symptoms. You are not alone, 1 in 20 online searches are health related and many live in fear of either having or about to develop a serious and life-threatening illness. Common sense suggests that a doctor can confirm or lay your fears to rest but people suffering from health anxiety avoid medical advice because they fear the diagnosis.

Health anxiety is associated with OCD as sufferers become obsessed with their health and seek continual reassurance. If they do go to the doctor and seek tests, they may not accept the result and demand a second or third opinion. The anxiety itself can consume and manifest itself in dizziness, headaches, fatigue, shaking, sweating and panic which makes the fear of illness worse.

Health anxiety became extremely real during lockdown when people were terrified to leave their houses and watched every news bulletin to check for updates on symptoms and death rates.

Understandably, if you have had a serious illness like cancer, there will probably be a fear that it will return but watch out for self-fulfilling prophecies.

Get checked out with your doctor or ring 111 and see **Tapping Stuff for** your fears.

132

Obviously not all health issues are stress related. The most common ones relating to student life are identified below.

Let's start with the dreaded lurgy – Covid 19. It is highly contagious and student living provides a ripe breeding ground. Be vigilant until we have all had the vaccine.

What to look for:

- High temperature

- New, continuous cough

- Change or loss to your sense of smell or taste

- Breathlessness

Your uni will have guidelines on what to do about reporting your symptoms but you will need to self-isolate and this can cause significant challenges which will inevitably be stressful. If you are in residential accommodation, there will be others around to make sure you are OK but if you are in independent places, it may be worth identifying a "buddy" who can bring you food and check you are recovering.

In the meantime:

- Get lots of rest

- Drink lots of water

- Take paracetamol or ibuprofen

- Take honey and lemon in hot water for the cough and sit upright to help breathing

- Try not to panic if you are breathless but do let someone know

Obviously, this is a new health issue for students but of course there are others that you need to look out for.

Meningitis

There are two types of meningitis – viral and bacterial, which is the more serious of the two. Bacterial meningitis causes inflammation of the brain lining and requires urgent medical treatment. Viral and bacterial meningitis have similar symptoms. Although it may be difficult to identify which type a person has, a doctor can often find out by doing tests.

What to look for:
• Fever
• Stiff neck
• Severe headache
• Eye sensitivity to light
• Vomiting
• Nausea
• Extreme sleepiness
• Confusion
• Seizure
• A rash that turns into purple blotches

www.meningitis.org
www.meningitisnow.org

Glandular fever

Glandular fever is very debilitating and can take a few months to go away, depending on the severity of the symptoms. It is passed on via saliva, coughs and sneezes, especially if you are run down. Once you have had it, you are immune from repeat infection.

What to look for:
• Flu like symptoms – fever and headaches
• Sore throat
• Swollen tonsils
• Swollen and hard glands in the armpit and groin

There is no medication available for glandular fever but do get a blood test to confirm diagnosis as you may need to go home for a complete rest to recover fully.
www.nhs.uk/conditions/glandular-fever

Mumps

This is generally thought of as a childhood illness, but it is surprisingly prevalent in students. Do check if you had the MMR vaccine as a child and if not, ask your doctor for it. Mumps is caught as easily as a cold but is much nastier!

What to look for:
- Swollen and painful face
- Headache
- Painful joints
- High temperature
- Loss of appetite

Mumps is highly contagious to those who have not been vaccinated and lasts 7-10 days. In rare cases it affects the inner ear and can cause deafness, or it can develop into meningitis.

Lots of rest, water, painkillers, and soft foods are all you can do as well as staying away from everyone! Quarantine for at least five – seven days after symptoms appear.

Chronic Fatigue Syndrome

Chronic fatigue syndrome (CFS) affects everyday life and doesn't go away with sleep or rest. It is an extremely debilitating condition which is often triggered by a viral infection or emotional distress.

CFS is also known as ME, which stands for myalgic encephalomyelitis.

CFS is a serious condition that can cause long-term illness and disability, but most people improve over time. Trouble is, it takes a long time to recover.

Paul had ME or CFS for five years from 11-16 and it was a long torturous journey back to health. It began just after he started secondary school when he had an irritable hip and couldn't walk. He was in hospital for a week then went back to school. Within a few weeks, he was ill again, this time it was suspected glandular fever. After a few months of total exhaustion, muscle weakness and loss of appetite, ME was diagnosed. His education over the next few years was a mixture of part-time school, home tuition and eventually hospital school. At 14 he needed to be carried to the loo as he was so weak. He was also tired all the time but couldn't sleep.

He could only go out in a wheelchair and felt very isolated and lonely. The only treatment that the hospital could offer was anti-depressants and physiotherapy. When he was 15, he had three sessions of hypnosis after which there were some signs of improvement. One of the identified causes had been the sudden and unexpected death of his granddad just before he had started high school. He managed to get four GCSEs at hospital school, went on to college and did some more plus A levels and ended up with a first-class degree in architecture from Oxford!

All of the above are horrid illnesses to have and prevention is better than cure - healthy eating, exercise and sleeping well can help physically.

See **Helpful Stuff** and **Tapping Stuff** to take care of your emotional health too.
www.meresearch.org.uk
www.actionforme.org.uk
www.meassociation.org.uk

Allergies

Allergies seem to be much more common now than ever before, but what are they? Most people with a healthy immune system are allergy free and find most substances harmless. When somebody is allergic to something, the immune system gets confused and thinks that the substance is bad for the body. The substances causing allergic reactions are known as allergens.

Some allergies develop in early childhood, but we grow out of them as our bodies develop immunity. Others can be controlled by medication.

Severe allergies can cause anaphylactic shock and even death. An anaphylactic shock is profoundly serious and needs a shot of adrenaline as soon as possible. Many people with allergies to things like bee stings or peanuts, carry an epi-pen which allows them to inject adrenaline as soon as they realise they have either eaten or come into contact with a known allergen.

The response to the allergy can be very quick and it affects the whole body. Normal allergy symptoms – runny nose, rash, itchy skin – can develop very rapidly to something much more serious, needing an ambulance and hospitalisation.

Knowing the symptoms could save someone's life, so keep your eyes open!
• The eyes or face have increasingly severe itching
• The mouth, throat, and tongue swell, making breathing and swallowing difficult
• Hives - a rash, itchy swollen and red skin
• Abdominal pain
• Cramps
• Vomiting
• Diarrhoea
• Tightness in chest causing shortness of breath and wheezing
• Confusion or dizziness

Often, we don't know that we are allergic until we experience a reaction. A good example of this is wasp stings. The easy solution is to stay clear of whatever causes the upset wherever possible. Having allergies can be incredibly stressful but generally speaking they are manageable.

sesame

fish pet hair oats

mustard gold milk eggs rye latex

wheat

washing powder soap barley dust strawberries

COMMON ALLERGIES

wasps

bees peanuts sea food soybeans celery perfume antibiotics

pollen

penicillin metals

nuts

SEXUALLY TRANSMITTED INFECTIONS

Sexually transmitted infections (STIs), are infections that are passed from person to person through sexual contact. (vaginal, anal, and oral sex).

Most people with STIs are unaware that they are infected, so are also unaware that they are passing the infection on. Some are more serious than others but can generally be treated effectively. However if they are left untreated, STIs can cause serious health problems including cervical cancer, liver disease, pelvic inflammatory disease(PID), infertility, and pregnancy problems.

Statistics show that many infections occur with 15-24 year olds, but not exclusively. With proper protection (or celibacy!) they can be avoided.

It is stressful for anyone to discover that s/he has an STI, especially if they are in a stable relationship (or thought they were!) It is also stressful and embarrassing to have to tell previous and present partners for all affected to be treated appropriately.

HIV

Human Immunodeficiency Virus is recognised as a disability. Unlike the Covid19 virus, it is not infectious in the same way.

The only way of being certain of being HIV positive is by having a test. Some newly infected people experience flu like symptoms known as seroconversion. Many put their symptoms down to flu and don't realise they have developed an immune deficiency.

HIV can be transmitted from one person to another through sexual contact and sharing needles and blood with an infected person.

Discovering that you are HIV positive is one thing, telling your partner is another. Both stressful and worrying – fear of rejection and relationship breakdowns create isolation and loneliness.

The stigma and fear of HIV that was around in the eighties has lessened, as has the risk of AIDS with proper medication.

Antiretroviral treatment (ART) suppresses viral replication but does not eliminate HIV and therefore treatment is lifelong. As previously stated, stress can depress the immune system and studies have shown that chronic stress, traumatic events, and depression can accelerate HIV disease progression

CONTRACEPTION, PREGNANCY & ABORTION

Many young women who are sexually active have an underlying fear of pregnancy, especially as it will disrupt or even destroy the chance of a good degree.

The stigma, shame and secrecy of using contraception is a thing of the past, and it is generally seen as common sense for young adults who are sexually active. However, for some young women, beliefs, fears and pressure stifle choice, which causes confusion and stress.

Realistically speaking, most people prefer to buy condoms in the chemist, supermarket or toilets rather than face embarrassing encounters with the doctor who looked after them when they had measles as a child! The pill is readily available on prescription and can help regulate periods. If you have unwanted side effects, change it to one that suits you. Do check out which contraception is right for you, there is plenty of choice!

Pregnancy tests can be bought quite cheaply (even in the pound shops!). It is wise to find out either way as soon as possible. Stressing can delay periods, regardless of pregnancy issues.

Signs and symptoms of pregnancy may include:
• Sore breasts
• Feeling sick or vomiting at any time of the day or night
• Feeling very tired
• Needing to wee often

Wherever the young woman goes, a doctor or nurse at the GP surgery or clinic will explain the options and where to get advice and independent counselling.

Unplanned pregnancy is undoubtedly stressful, and some young women feel unable to continue with it. Did we really believe any of the myths or old wives' tales (that are still around) like bringing on a miscarriage by jumping up and down or having a hot bath and drinking loads of gin?

If there is any risk of pregnancy after having unprotected sex, then young women may appreciate advice on the morning after pill as soon as possible. It is available in most pharmacies, but it must be paid for. Sexual health clinics offer it for free, as do some GP surgeries.

If the pregnancy was a mistake but the couple are in a stable relationship, then partner support can help with the decision-making.

The options are generally to have the child, have a termination or have the baby adopted after birth.

Most abortions in England and Wales are done in the first 13 weeks (three months). The earlier the better. If there is no steady relationship, then many young women turn to their families and friends for support.

It can be hard for a young woman to admit to being pregnant, to both the father and their families who may be disappointed at the termination of studies and career prospects.

Mistakes and accidents happen. The first sign of pregnancy is usually a missed period, and many then start to worry rather than checking out for sure.

In order to get an abortion on the NHS a doctor's referral is required. There are usually three stages to this process.

1. The doctor makes a referral to the NHS abortion service. If the young woman is under 25, they can also go to a young people's service such as Brook.

2. An assessment appointment will be held at the clinic or hospital where the abortion will be carried out. The doctor or nurse will explain the different types of abortion and will talk things over with the young woman.

3. She will be given another appointment at the hospital or clinic to have the abortion.

There are also independent abortion providers such as bpas (the British Pregnancy Advisory Service) or Marie Stopes UK, which can provide abortions on the NHS as well as private abortions which are paid for.

PAIN

In our society we tend to deal with the symptoms of physical ill health rather than the causes. We wait until we have a pain and then take a painkiller which masks the symptoms and can possibly make the condition worse.

Arguably pain is telling us that something is wrong or that the body is damaged in some way.

This is easy to accept when we have broken an arm or leg but what about pain without any obvious damage? Psychosomatic pain is real and happens when mental and emotional triggers cause physical symptoms, but without any physical disease. Have you ever noticed that when you are stressed or uptight, your physical "weak spot" manifests itself in some way? My hearing declines and when I am very tired, or my ankle will twitch and ache. I have broken it three times.

Mind over matter can work, but not all the time. I amazed myself at a Tony Robbins event when I did the fire walk. Walking barefoot over hot coals whilst telling myself it was cool wet grass is something that I would not have believed if I hadn't done it for myself!

Louise Hay, in her book "You can Heal Your Life" links certain emotions to specific illnesses. She advocates forgiveness for self-healing and releasing the past. The same message with more scientific evidence is portrayed in "The Body Keeps the Score" by Bessel Van Der Kolk.

When I was in my mid- twenties, I developed a chronic pain condition, it was one of those things that baffled numerous doctors and I ended up having to take nerve suppressing medication. 4 years on and I'd been to places much darker than I ever knew existed, my worst point being at the start of this year when I thought I may have to give up work because even the strongest medication wasn't helping. And then, I met Ruth. Without her I really don't know what shape my life would be in right now. I don't really understand how EFT is so powerful but somehow Ruth and her EFT skills have transformed my life.

I remember the first time I saw Ruth, and I remember the black cloud that followed me in through her front door. I was depressed, (undiagnosed) and suffering so much that I just couldn't cope anymore. I woke up in pain and went to bed in pain and I avoided seeing friends because my mind was so consumed by it all. When I did see people, I felt absent, like an imposter had taken over my body and was pretending to be me. Within a few sessions with Ruth I was back at work full time and reducing my medication. I started saying yes to nights out and invited people over. At work, I held my head up high instead of hanging it low and instead of looking exhausted and worn down I found my smile again. Pretty soon everyone noticed the changes in me. It was like the real me had finally woken up and tunnelled a way out of the pain. I had my life back.

Yesterday I completed an 8-mile midnight charity walk and I'm feeling great. I may have lost several years of my life to this condition but now I'm back, I'm me again and if I ever feel that black cloud creeping in again, I'll be knocking at Ruth's door because I know that's where I'll find the sunshine. Alison H.

Eating disorders and weight issues

Obesity is one of the greatest health hazards in the UK.

Food acts so efficiently to mask negative feelings that we don't want to experience, that we may not recognise the connections. "Emotional Eating" is now recognised by scientists and doctors as a reality. We overeat to suppress feelings, reduce stress, and change moods. It acts as a temporary tranquilliser. Eating disorders and weight issues are very rarely about food! Most young adults worry about how they look – many strive to look like skinny models that are in magazines, social media and on TV.

We all need food to survive and we have so much food available to us it is hard to choose between what is healthy and good for our bodies and what we fancy. Family meals around the table seem to be a thing of the past; instead we eat on trays in front of the television. Fast food and ready meals are replacing good old-fashioned home cooking. Who really knows what is in those packages? What percentage of your diet is fast food? Students may be forgiven for eating more fast food than the rest of us but it costs so much more than fresh food which is also more eco friendly without all the packaging.

We know that in the UK, we are unlikely to starve, but the pandemic has raised awareness of those who do not have enough to eat. Foodbanks and food parcels have become commonplace as people lose their jobs, income and in some places their homes as well.

Obesity is probably the greatest health hazard that we face in the UK, (apart from Covid-19) and although the government is now wise to the damage of sugar, the NHS is trying to cope with the aftermath of post war sugar consumption. The diet industry is worth millions; books, DVDs, clubs, and workouts all recommend something different, so which do you choose to follow?

The main problem is that little is explained as to why we want to overeat on certain things. Sugar is physically addictive and poor eating has become a habit.

Like all habits, as you have seen in **Mind Stuff**, eating habits are learned and practised until they become automatic. The conscious mind is no longer in control, and has handed over to its partner, the subconscious, where the habit is programmed. We are on auto pilot..... which controls what, when, where and how we eat!

Subconsciously we have all trained our minds and bodies to eat certain foods at certain times in certain ways, so now we no longer think about it.

Think back to growing up and see if any of the statements below are true for you.

- You were expected to eat everything on your plate.
- You had to eat your food before you could go out to play or leave the table.
- You were not allowed pudding or dessert if you hadn't eaten all your vegetables.
- You celebrated birthdays and special occasions with food (parties, meals out, cakes).
- If you fell over or were upset, you were rewarded with a sweet or chocolate.
- If you did something special at school, you were rewarded at home with food and drink.
- You had regular mealtimes – whether you were hungry or not.
- Now that you are older do you:
- Raid the fridge when you are bored?
- Treat yourself to a meal out?
- Eat for comfort?
- Eat when you are lonely, sad, nervous, bored…?

Food acts so efficiently to mask feelings that we don't want to experience, that we may not recognise the connections. We know that in the UK, we are unlikely to starve, so why do we eat as if there was going to be no food left for tomorrow?

"Emotional Eating" is now recognised by scientists and doctors as a reality. This is overeating to suppress feelings, reduce stress and change moods. Here are just a few of the situations that can trigger emotional overeating.

For many people food is a major tranquilliser. This is one of the reasons why so many people develop an addiction to certain "favourite" foods - they act just like a medicine.Overeating, or eating when you are full and the body no longer has a real need for food, is like filling up a car petrol tank and then proceeding to fill the back and front seats with petrol too. Why, if we don't need any more food as fuel, do we continue to eat?

People who lose weight on diets will almost always gain it back unless they have identified the deep anxieties and conflicts that led them to develop the habit of using food to numb their feelings in the first place.

Some people, however, are just naturally greedy or unaware of what is good for their bodies and what is not. Fast food chains provide convenience, not health.

Overeating is not actually recognised as an eating disorder, but it does just as much damage as those we are familiar with.

The best-known eating disorders are often started in student years:
• Anorexia Nervosa
• Bulimia
• Binge Eating Disorder

Anorexia Nervosa

Anorexia is very serious and is potentially life-threatening. Sufferers of anorexia tend to be obsessive about weight, appearance and body image.

Someone with anorexia will see themselves in the mirror as a size sixteen when they are really a ten. They believe that they are fat and are determined to lose weight at any cost. This body image is usually accompanied by low confidence and self-esteem.

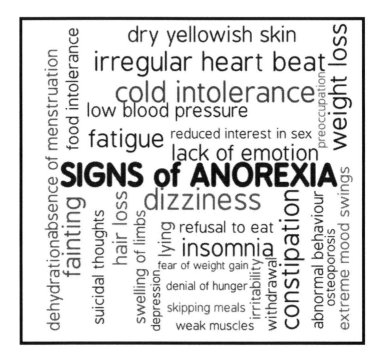

Sufferers believe that they will be happier, more popular, and more attractive if they are slimmer – at any cost. Most people with anorexia have low confidence and poor self-esteem. They see their weight loss as the only thing to make them feel better, and this provides a sense of control. It is a form of self-harm, and starvation results in loss of muscle strength and reduced bone strength in women and girls.   With boys and young men it can affect sexual ability.

Lack of understanding from friends and family can prompt withdrawal and poor performance at university/college.

Long term effects
- Weakens immune system and resistance to illness
- Problems with physical growth and development
- Risk of osteoporosis (loss of bone density)
- Potential infertility

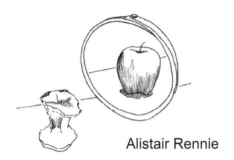

Alistair Rennie

Bulimia

People with bulimia nervosa tend to binge on food and then feel so guilty that they try to compensate or try to get rid of what they have eaten by deliberately making themselves vomit or by taking too many laxatives.

Like anorexia, bulimia mainly affects young women and begins during adolescence or early adulthood. Statistics show that about half of those with anorexia go on to have bulimia. Not nice!

There are no obvious physical signs or symptoms of bulimia, such as sudden weight loss, so it may be harder to detect than anorexia. Constant vomiting and diarrhoea can obviously lead to dehydration and loss of the minerals and nutrients we all need.

Abusing Laxatives
Obsession with Appearance
Lack of Concentration   Insomnia
Forced vomiting
Craves attention   Mood Swings
BULIMIA
Needs acceptance   Sexual promiscuity
Shame   Depression
          Irritability
Body Image Preoccupation   Guilt
Alcohol/Drug abuse

Long-Term Effects
- Dehydration (which can lead to kidney failure)
- Hormone imbalance (which can cause fertility and menstrual problems)
- Tearing of the throat, oesophagus and stomach
- Palpitations and irregular heartbeat
- Exhaustion
- Bowel problems
- As you can see, there are a lot of similarities between the two but it is generally believed that all eating disorders have an emotional link or trigger.

Binge Eating Disorder
Binge eating is also an illness with devastating long-term effects on your wellbeing.

Unlike anorexics who avoid food, binge eaters are compulsive eaters who binge when they are upset about something, so they overeat to compensate. However, this is followed by guilt, shame, anger, and hopelessness. This condition is also called compulsive overeating, emotional eating, or food addiction. There seems to be no control over knowing when to stop eating, and the person affected eats more and more until they are absolutely stuffed. They then feel guilty and depressed so eat again for comfort and solace. This condition differs from bulimia because there is no forced vomiting or excessive use of laxatives.

Food is their invisible friend. Most binge eaters are at risk of type two diabetes and other issues relating to being overweight and can put a strain on muscles and organs.

For further information:
www.beateatingdisorders.org.uk/support-services/ helplines
www.nhs.uk/conditions/eating-disorders/

SMOKING

Historically, smoking was believed to calm nerves and relieve stress....

Lots of us start smoking in teenage years, either as a dare, because of peer pressure, or because friends and parents do. As you may know, it quickly becomes a very expensive habit.

Tobacco came into the UK in Elizabethan times and it was believed that it "calmed the nerves" so much so that during both world wars, the troops were given cigarettes as part of their rations.

The health risks and hazards started to emerge in the 1950's when it was realised what the contents of cigarettes could do. The most damage is caused by nicotine, but they also contain other poisons – tar, carbon monoxide, oxidant gasses, benzene and polonium.

So, what does it do to us?

Nicotine

When you smoke, nicotine affects your brain within seconds of inhaling. The heart rate increases and causes a surge in the hormones noradrenalin and dopamine in your brain. This has a positive effect on your mood and your ability to concentrate. However, in between cigarettes, these hormone levels drop, leaving you feeling irritable, anxious and in need of another cigarette.

Within 24 hours, withdrawal from nicotine can cause the following side effects:
As well as being addictive, nicotine can be dangerous if you have high blood pressure. It increases the risk of a sudden rise in already-high blood pressure that can cause headaches, blurred vision and vomiting.

Nicotine also slows down your body's ability to heal itself by making your skin dehydrated. However, other substances found in cigarettes are far more dangerous.

Diseases caused or made worse by smoking
Lung cancer - 8 out of 10 cases of lung cancer deaths are directly related to smoking.

Emphysema and Chronic Obstructive Pulmonary Disease (COPD) are painful and serious lung diseases and 8 out of 10 of deaths from this condition are directly linked to smoking.

Heart disease is the biggest killer illness in the UK and 1 in 7 deaths are attributed to smoking.

Other cancers - of the mouth, nose, throat, larynx, oesophagus, pancreas, bladder, cervix, blood and kidneys are all more common in smokers.

Circulation. The chemicals in tobacco can damage the lining of the blood vessels and affect the level of fats in the bloodstream which contributes to the hardening of the arteries. This is the main cause of heart disease.

Ageing- Smokers tend to develop more 'lines' on their face at an earlier age than non-smokers. This often makes smokers look older than they really are.

Fertility is reduced in smokers (both male and female). Children and babies who live in a smoking household are more likely to get chest infections and asthma and are at greater risk of cot death. They are more vulnerable to chest infections in later life.

Passive smoking

Anyone who is exposed to cigarette smoke on a long-term basis has an increased risk of lung cancer and heart disease.

These may all seem a long way off but as with all things, prevention is better than cure.

David started smoking when he was eighteen and although he had given up several times over the years, he always started again when he was under stress. He became a heavy smoker after a motorcycle accident in which he killed a four-year-old child. It was unavoidable as the child ran out into the road in front of him. The coroner however was quite intimidating and critical of young drivers.

He used smoking as a coping strategy to come to terms with this tragedy. The pattern became established and his subconscious mind made the link between stress and smoking, prompting him to light up when under pressure or challenged by his boss. He was fascinated as we unpacked his past and cleared all the painful and uncomfortable memories. He is now a non-smoker.

Smoking is covered in **Tapping Stuff** but here are a few tips as well.

STOP SMOKING TIPS

- **Decide** *on your target date to be a non - smoker*

- **Write** *down the benefits of stopping*

- **Think** *about how many you smoke a day - which ones can you cut out first?*

- **Go** *public - tell friends you are quitting*

- **Ask** *smoking friends not to offer you any*

- **Keep** *your mouth and hands busy when you normally smoke*

- **Try** *and have tea, coffee, wine, beer without a cigarette*

- **Delay** *each cigarette*

- **Stop** *the habitual ones - on the phone, driving etc.*

- **Tap** *for the cravings - see Tapping Stuff*

- **Make** *an appointment with a hypnotherapist*

ALCOHOL

Like smoking, drinking alcohol has a long history. In fact it goes back more than 10,000 years!

Having an occasional drink is not a problem, but binge drinking and alcoholism is. If you have ever had a hangover you will know it is very unpleasant!

Alcohol is of course legal in the UK – maybe if it was discovered today it would not be, as it is linked to heart disease, stroke risk, blood pressure and a range of cancers. It affects memories and brain cells and is certainly not a cure for stress!

Drinking, smoking, having sex for the first time and leaving home are all markers on the transition from childhood to the adult world. Sadly, very few of us make informed choices, we go with the flow to be accepted by our peer group or improve our perception of ourselves.

Student bar prices are usually cheaper than the average pub so it can be tempting to drink. Read on!

Alcohol facts and figures

- More than 9 million people in England drink more than the recommended daily limits.
- Alcohol accounts for 10% of death and disease in the UK, making alcohol the biggest health risk for disease after smoking and obesity.
- An estimated 7.5 million people are unaware of the damage their drinking could be causing.
- Alcohol related harm costs billions of pounds – damage to property, the costs to the NHS as well as lost working days.
- Alcohol is 61% more affordable now than it was thirty years ago!
- Alcohol contributes to more than 60 medical conditions, including mouth, throat, stomach, liver and breast cancers; high blood pressure, cirrhosis of the liver; and depression.
- The number of young people between the ages of 15-19 admitted to hospitals in England with mental and behavioural disorders associated with alcohol use has risen by 94% in the past ten years.

We get warnings about the number of units we should have in a week but that is meaningless to many of us. Have a look at the table at **www.drinkaware.co.uk**

If you are struggling to cut down on your consumption, use EFT to reduce the craving and stay in control.

See **Tapping Stuff**
www.alcoholconcern.org.uk
www.talktofrank.com/drug/alcohol
www.nhs.uk/Livewell/alcohol
www.dontbottleitup.org.uk

I always chuckle when I think of this client who came to see me to explore his increase in drinking wine. I had seen his wife some months before for grief when her dad had had died so I knew the family circumstances.

We quickly got the wine under control but the following week when Paul came, he said that whilst he had no interest in wine, he was now on beer! When that was under control, he went onto spirits!

The one circumstance that I was unaware of was that his wife's mother was now living with them and that was the problem. The drinking was Paul's way of trying to cope with the change in the dynamics at home and his feelings about it. When we worked through these, he stopped drinking.

DRINKING TIPS

- **Eat first -** *food slows down the absorption of alcohol into the blood stream*

- **Stay well hydrated -** *drink water with your meal and if you can, in between drinks. This can help to prevent headaches the next day.*

- **Plan your transport in advance -** *if you know you are going to make a night of it, arrange a taxi or lift to ensure you arrive home safely.*

- **Stay with your friends -** *if you have had too much to drink, you are more vulnerable to muggers, pickpockets and worse.*

- **Pace yourself -** *Don't drink too much too quickly and miss out on the fun by passing out or vomiting.*

- **Choose your drinks carefully and don't mix them.** *Watch out for the shots, they can make you drunk very quickly.*

- **Don't accept drinks from strangers -** *spiked drinks from strangers can put you at risk.*

- **Cheat! -** *stay sober by drinking "mocktails" or non-alcoholic beer, wine and soft drinks.*

- **Have fun being safe and (reasonably) sober!**

DRUGS

A stereotypical student has long hair, goes travelling in the holidays, attends protest marches, is promiscuous, likes music, drinks, smokes and takes drugs. Does this describe you?! I doubt it! Many students do experiment with drugs because they have the opportunity to so and they are accessible. Why do you need or want them?

An NUS Students Drug Survey was carried out in 2018 to explore of students' attitudes to, and experiences of, drugs. 2,810 students took part and discovered that most of the respondents mainly used drugs for recreational purposes (80 %). 39 % used drugs for social reasons and 3% to relieve stress. Other motivations were to improve confidence, cope with a difficult life event or enhance sex.
Of course, this was pre Covid-19 and undoubtedly stress levels amongst students have increased, so has drug usage?

Over half of the respondents admitted to using drugs and 94% of these had used cannabis regularly. Ecstasy / MDMA was used by 67% and nitrous oxide and cocaine had been used by half of the group.

The majority of students did not see drug use as a problem and felt safe taking them. They did however admit to them affecting their studies or attendance at lectures. There was a mixed response as to whether drugs improved or damaged physical and mental health. The jury is still out regarding legalising Cannabis in the UK. In the meantime – whatever you decide to take, check it out first and stay safe.

www.talktofrank.com
www.nhs.uk/Livewell/drugs

Other effects of stress on the body
"The link between stress and increased risk of developing heart disease has previously focused on the lifestyle habits people take up when they feel stressed such as smoking, drinking too much alcohol and overeating."
British Heat Foundation

High Blood pressure, heart attacks, strokes and some cancers have evidenced links to stress as do
• Menopause (male and female)
• PMT- Premenstrual Tension
• PMDD - Premenstrual Dysphoric Disorder
• Musculoskeletal issues (muscle tension and pain)
• Respiratory problems
• Gastrointestinal matters (including IBS)
• Crohn's Disease and Ulcerative Colitis
• Skin problems (eczema, psoriasis, spots)
• Type 2 Diabetes
• Sexual desire
• Conception

" To keep your body in good health is a duty – otherwise we shall not be able to keep our minds sharp and clear"
Buddha

This summarises this chapter well and developing healthy habits as a young adult during student years is one of the best investments you can make for your future.

6

CHALLENGING

STUFF

"Life's challenges are not supposed to paralyse you – they are supposed to help you discover who you are"
Bernice Johnson Reagon

This lovely quotation applies to everyone who has overcome the challenges that life presented them with.
We are not talking about the challenge of running a marathon or climbing a mountain here, but it is a much nicer word than "problem". Challenge implies that there is a way forward for us to learn from the experience and grow as individuals.

This however implies that we have a choice about the challenges we face but of course that is not always true, so this chapter explores challenging times which may affect us all at some point.

However, there are some challenges that are common to students, primarily exams and interviews for placements, internships and eventually jobs.

Assuming that you are familiar with your learning style (visual, auditory, or kinaesthetic), it is probably best to choose this method to revise. Beware of procrastination or putting things off until the last minute. Brian Tracey, an American motivational speaker, wrote a great book called "Eat that Frog." where he advises that we eat the biggest frog first because after that, the others will slide down more easily! Yuck! What he is really saying of course is that if we deal with the subject that causes us the most anxiety or stress first, then the others will seem easy. If we do it the other way round, then the "big frog" is hanging around all day.

REVISION TIPS

- **Plan** *well ahead and draw up a revision plan*

- **Stick** *to it!*

- **Choose** *a place where you won't be disturbed*

- **Explore** *what works best for you – notes, index cards, mind maps video tutorials etc*

- **Check** *out anything you don't understand with a tutor before you learn the wrong thing.*

- **Talk** *to someone about any concerns before they get out of proportion.*

- **Study** *old exam papers and go through them.*

- **Eat** *healthy food and drink lots of water.*

- **Get** *plenty of sleep.*

- **TAP** *for any emotional blockages. See* **Tapping Stuff**

- **Pace** *yourself and don't try to do every subject at once.*

- **Take** *regular breaks*

- **Get** *some exercise and fresh air*

- **Plan** *in some fun*

- **Believe** *in yourself*

- **Consider** *having a Study Buddy for accountability*

If you have any bad memories from previous exams - see **Tapping Stuff** to clear them so that you are not carrying any unnecessary or additional anxiety with you into the exam room.

You are probably aware of the following Tips, but they are always worth a reminder!

EXAM TIPS

- **Get** a good night's sleep before each exam

- **Have** a good breakfast – fuel to keep your energy levels up

- **TAP** for nerves. see **Tapping Stuff**

- **Arrive** in plenty of time

- **Don't** listen to your friends if they are stressing

- **Go** to the loo before going into the exam room

- **Take** a bottle of water with you (dehydration causes confusion)

- **When** the exam starts, take a couple of deep breaths and read the instructions carefully

- **Work** out how long you have for each question allowing time to check your answer.

- **Prioritise** your questions, easiest first.

- **Underline** the key words of the question.

- **Don't** rush but keep an eye on the time.

- **If** you get "brain freeze" – stop for a moment, close your eyes and breathe deeply.

- **When** you have finished, read your answers through, checking for grammar errors.

- **After** the exam, try and avoid "post-mortems" or dwelling on what you could have said differently.

- **Go** and chill – you deserve it!

INTERVIEWS

Getting an interview for a placement, internship or job can be nerve racking and stressful. We imagine all sorts of scenarios about the building, the interviewers, the questions and inevitably the answers!

If you attend the university "milk rounds", be mindful that the "stall holders" will be assessing you and first impressions are vitally important. Think of the questions you want to ask them in advance and find out as much as you can about the company too.

Most interviews include a presentation which can cause anxiety about making mistakes, a fear of being judged or forgetting our words. This is linked to a fear of making fools of ourselves by showing our stress by shaking or having complete brain freeze.

Glossophobia is the fear of public speaking and it usually goes back to an uncomfortable memory from childhood. Making a mistake reading out loud in class which prompts laughter is enough for your mind to register the embarrassment and discomfort. These feelings are triggered or reactivated in similar situations by the subconscious.

You can however tap out the feelings and memories to put you in control when you need to be. See **Tapping Stuff**

INTERVIEW TIPS

- **Find** out as much as you can about the job / course / company beforehand

- **Think** about the sort of questions you might be asked and prepare your answers (and any questions)

- **Have** a mock interview with a friend

- **Rehearse** your answers

- **Dress** smartly

- **Tap** for any nerves before you go in

- **Don't** be late

- **Shake** the interviewer's hand when you go in (If you can)

- **Smile** and look relaxed (they will be watching your body language)

- **Practice** and check spelling and grammar on slides or handouts if you are doing a presentation

- **Speak** clearly and make eye contact

- **Do** not be afraid to ask for clarity or a repeat of the question

- **Take** a breath before answering

- **Look** positive and show them how keen you are

- **Don't** answer with yes or no if you can expand your answer

- **Try** to avoid saying "um", "er", and "you know"

- **Ask** questions when invited – what do you need to know?

- **Check** when they will let you know the outcome if you have not been told

- **Thank** them for seeing you at the end of the interview

GOOD LUCK!

ABUSE

Abuse is a major safety issue within our society, but many young adults who were abused as children, accept it as their norm. For some, sadly, they did not know anything different.

Recent cases of exposure, modern slavery, grooming and violation of young women and children have made the public realise how big an issue it is.

"Abuse is a violation of an individual's human and civil rights by any other person or persons." Home Office 2000
Many people, however, do not realise that there are different types of abuse, each of which can be extremely stressful and cause long-term mental health damage to the individual.

Society generally abhors abusers of any kind and many would argue that the perpetrators are the ones with a mental health problem,

NEGLECT

SEXUAL ABUSE   **PHYSICAL ABUSE**

EMOTIONAL ABUSE

Hopefully, you have not been a victim of abuse yourself, so the following signs and symptoms may help you to identify abuse or the effects of it, in the future. Many victims of abuse are too scared to tell anyone for fear of the possible consequences.

The effects of abuse are soul destroying and long lasting.

Neglect
- Being left alone for long periods of time as a child
- Always hungry
- Dirty or smelly
- Weight loss
- Inappropriate dress

Julie lacked confidence and felt inadequate in everything she did. She believed that her parents loved her sister more than her but did not understand why she felt like this as she had no evidence to support her feelings. In regression in hypnosis, she recalled that at the age of five, she was left alone all night at home when her sister was being born in hospital. She was terrified and this became worse as she got a bit older as her parents would go out at night, leaving her to look after her sister. The fear she experienced then was carried into adult life because of the neglect as a child.

Physical Abuse
This is a deliberate act and is usually delivered through hitting, shaking, throwing, poisoning, burning or scalding, drowning, suffocating or otherwise causing physical harm.
It is often easier to identify by unexplained bruises, bruises which reflect hand marks, cigarette burns, bite marks, broken bones, or scalds. This form of abuse can cause changes in behaviour, fear, aggression, and depression. This type of abuse can be experienced by us all, regardless of age and gender.

Emotional Abuse
Continuous emotional ill treatment of another person can also cause severe mental health issues. It is harder to see in someone else but occurs when a person feels worthless or unloved and shows itself in a fear of making mistakes, self-harm, stammering, lack of confidence, low self-esteem, and body image.
Most emotional abuse is verbal and intricately linked to bullying.

It can take the form of:
- Intimidation, threats, and humiliation
- Racial, sexual, or homophobic abuse
- Harassment, coercion, and extortion
- Being isolated from people other than the abuser and from other sources of information
- Being made to say or do things out of fear
- Being deprived of sleep, being kept exhausted and debilitated
- Having one's sense of reality distorted by misinformation and lies
- Misuse of medication
- Deprivation of privacy and other human rights
- Lack of access to social activities
- Continual rejection

Pamela was five when her parents split up. Neither she nor her brother really knew why but as she got older, she realised that her dad was keeping in contact with her brother but not her. Her dad remarried and lived in the States, had more children but still Pamela was not contacted. She was welcomed by her stepmother and went to stay but never received a hug or smile from her father.

She felt totally rejected and hurt, and this manifested itself in her believing that she was not good enough and it was something that she did that caused her parents to split. Her self-esteem and self-image were exceptionally low, and that resulted in her struggling to make healthy relationships as an adult.

Child Sexual Abuse
This aspect of abuse is the most known, and like the others can have long-lasting effects. Sexual abuse is forcing or enticing a child or young person to take part in sexual activities, whether the child or young person is aware of, or consents to what's happening.
It includes:
- Penetrative acts; rape, buggery, oral sex

- Non-penetrative; fondling and touching
- Non-contact – involving children/young people in looking at pornographic material or watching sexual acts

If you have been a victim of sexual abuse – It is never too late to report it. The perpetrator may have found another victim now that you have left home.
Everybody needs to understand that they have a responsibility to share what they know. Most victims disclose when they really do need help and secretly want something to happen to make it stop. Disclosure can also bring closure to the situation.

Mary was 14 and at boarding school when her best friend told her that she was made to have sex on a regular basis with her dad at weekends. Mary was upset and didn't know what to do so she told her mum. Mum rang the school and the police went round and arrested the dad who was then convicted on various counts including having illegal sex with an underage girl. It transpired that the mum was disabled and could not meet her husband's sexual needs and was aware of what was going on. Mary's friend meanwhile was incredibly angry with Mary for telling her mum. She didn't speak to Mary again and this in turn distressed Mary so much, she attempted suicide. Mary's mum brought her to see me to unravel the anger, hurt, confusion and guilt that Mary was experiencing.

***

Alan was bought up in a children's home because his mother couldn't cope. His brother was adopted but Alan wasn't which caused a lot of resentment and low self-esteem. The only place he felt wanted and needed by anyone was in the choir at his local church. He was sexually abused by the curate and although he hated it and was ashamed, he craved the attention.
He grew up and became a successful businessman but never told anyone about the abuse. He mentored and trained a young man who he became fond of until he

170

discovered that he had been stealing from him over a period (over £100,000).

Alan's confidence and faith in human nature plummeted and all the childhood feelings came back – lack of confidence, anger, shame, despair.

During therapy he finally disclosed his abuse and was able to acknowledge the effect it had on him. He carried his secret for fifty years.

Most victims of abuse tell a friend first, but others find it easier to tell a stranger about what has happened rather than someone they are close to. Specially trained counsellors are available on telephone help lines that can talk with them about what has happened and provide support to help make sure that they are safe. They will also advise on what to do next.

A professional who has some distance from the situation can offer objective advice and guidance.
Many victims avoid making an allegation against a family member, because they doubt that they will be believed and also know how disruptive the disclosure will be to the family.

Your uni should be able to advise you on the best way forward.

DOMESTIC VIOLENCE
Domestic violence is also abuse and can happen to anyone. During lockdown, the Met Police made an average of nearly 100 arrests every day for domestic abuse offences. Staying at home caused stress and anxiety for those who lived in fear or were at risk. Everyone should feel safe and secure in their own home. We all need to have control over our choices and decisions and maintain self-respect, self-esteem, and self-worth. Being deprived of

these can cause emotional, physical and social scars which can last a lifetime.

Domestic abuse is all about control and it is sometimes so subtle, that the victim is unaware of what is happening, until it becomes unbearable. It can take many forms – not just physical violence – hitting, slapping, beating and kicking. The other types of abuse are covered by the term Coercive Control which is a criminal offence. It carries a maximum penalty of five years' imprisonment and a fine.

The legislation closes a gap around patterns of coercive and controlling behaviour in relationships between:
• intimate partners
• former partners who still live together
• family members.

It covers the following behaviours towards the victim:
• Isolation from family and friends
• Monitoring and restricting online communication tools such as social media
• Controlling   everyday life, where they can go, who they can see or talk to, what to wear and when to sleep
• Deprivation of access to support services, including medical help.
• Repeatedly intimidating, humiliating, undermining, and ridiculing them
• Enforcement of behaviour which is degrading and dehumanising
• Threatening children as a way of preventing disclosure to authorities
• Prevention of access to transport, employment, or education
• Withdrawal of financial or economic support
• Continuous sexual abuse
You may think that this doesn't apply to you, but ITV news recently reported on young women who had been abused and murdered by ex-boyfriends.
No-one knows what goes on behind closed doors, but lockdown kept those doors closed far longer than normal.

The help websites have **Exit Site** signs so that anyone caught researching can escape the site quickly if they are interrupted.

Most domestic abuse victims are women, but men can be victims too. Recognising that you may be a victim of domestic abuse is one thing – having the courage to break away is another.

Keep a record of everything that happens to you for evidence and contact the following:

www.nationaldahelpline.org.uk

www.met.police.uk/advice/advice-and-information/daa/ domestic-abuse/what-is-domestic-abuse

Fortunately, there is plenty of help online and practitioners will advise a victim on how to keep information in relation to incidents and themselves safe.

24 Hour National Domestic Violence Helpline is run in partnership with Women's Aid and Refuge on 0808 2000247

Some victims put up with abuse because their self-esteem is so low that they blame themselves and think that they deserve everything they get. It is a form of brainwashing and common emotions are:

• Hopelessness
• Feeling unworthy
• Apprehensive and discouraged about the future
• Inability to trust
• Questioning and doubting spiritual faith
• Unmotivated

Some victims believe that their partners will change and live in hope. Change can happen but the issues need to be dealt with professionally and with willingness on behalf of both partners.

It is not unusual for victims to suffer PTSD, prolonged anxiety, and loss of self-worth.

Pami is an attractive Asian woman in her early forties. She came to see me because she said she had experienced a breakdown the previous weekend. She was married with two children and lived in a nice house by the river.

However, she "was not good enough" for her husband and felt totally worthless and could not see the point in living. With some gentle questioning, it transpired that her sister had died when she was 15 of cancer. She had lived in the shadow of her sister's illness for eight years and always felt that she was of no value. At the funeral, she overheard an aunt saying that "the beautiful one has gone now" This did not help her self-esteem or body image.

She defied her culture and married for love at 22 but his parents have for the last twenty years, belittled her, saying that her skin is not fair enough, and that she is a lousy mother because she doesn't give her children Indian food all the time.

It gradually emerged that this brow beating was coming from her husband too. He would speak to his parents in India, morning and night, criticising and moaning about his wife. Whatever they said to him, he would pass on to Pami in a derogatory tone. He did not however want a divorce and when Pami raised it, he refused to consider it. At the beginning of lockdown, she lost her job as a banker and she felt trapped and desperate to escape – either to be with her sister and grandmother in heaven or to a life without her husband and his family.

Her mother (in the USA) did not understand and said that all marriages go through hiccups and she just had to get on with it. Pami was better educated and more travelled than her husband and his family but she was so low and believed whatever her husband was saying to her.

Over the years she had become brainwashed into believing that she was not likable, let alone lovable but when challenged she realised that maybe this was not true. We looked for evidence of her not being liked outside her husband's family and there wasn't any. Having cleared the painful memories that had been haunting her and rebuilding her confidence, she started to plan and explore options for an in independent life.

FGM

This is an abhorrent form of abuse within our culture but still acceptable in others. It is illegal in the UK. It is part of the Serious Crime Act and is included in the Safeguarding Agenda. It is applicable to females between and five and fifteen and in some cultures is believed to control female sexuality, and ensure virginity before marriage and fidelity afterward, as well as increasing male sexual pleasure.

Female Genital Mutilation is carried out without any medical justification, often without anaesthetic by a non-medically trained woman. It can be done with knives, scissors, scalpels, pieces of glass or razor blades and some die from blood loss. Most children and young women are held down forcibly as the procedure is against their wishes.

Not only does the experience cause many cases of PTSD but also creates physical problems in later life. They may be in constant pain, have difficulty in having sex, be incontinent, have infections which can lead to infertility or problems during labour and birth.

NSPCC helpline 0808 800 5000
help@nspcc.org
www.childline.org.uk

RAPE

One of the most challenging things that can happen to any one of us, is rape which can destroy personal confidence and self-esteem.

When most of us think about rape we tend to assume that a stranger jumps out of a shadowy place and attacks their victim. In reality, about half of all people who are raped know the person who attacked them.

Rape is defined if a man (usually) intentionally penetrates the vagina, mouth or anus of another person, male or female with his penis without that person's consent or if they are under 13, (young people aged 12 and under are not legally able to give consent to any sexual activity).

Girls and women are more likely to be raped, but it can also happen to boys and young men. It's not just men who rape. In rare cases, women rape, too. The rape of children is too horrendous to contemplate but it does happen, and we all need to be vigilant and report any concerns to Social Services and the police.

Rape facts
The person who gets raped is not to blame.
Rape is always the rapist's fault. People never "ask for it" because of the clothes they wear or the way they act. If sex is forced against someone's will, it's rape. That's true even when two people are dating or married — even if they've had sex before. You never "owe" someone sex, even if you're a couple.

Rape is not always violent.
If you say "no," but the person doesn't respect your wishes and talks you into something that you don't want, it's rape.

Rape is not about sex or passion.
Forced sex is an act of violence and aggression. It has nothing to do with love. Healthy relationships are about respect. Someone who really cares about another will respect their partner's wishes and not force or pressure them to do anything sexual without agreement.

Date rape
This is a topic that is usually, but not always associated with young people. It refers to forced sex that can happen on a date but also somewhere like a party or at a club with someone the victim may know, like, or even be interested in.

Alcohol and drugs often contribute to date rapes. Drinking can loosen inhibitions, reduce common sense, and, for some people, allow aggressive tendencies to surface. They take away self-control and when mixed into other drinks are almost impossible to detect.

The well-known (dangerous) drugs associated with date rape are:
• **Rohypnol**, called roofies, lunch money, or mind erasers.
• **GHB** (gamma hydroxybutyric acid), called cherry meth, energy drink, gook.
• **Ketamine**, called bump, special K, and super acid.

Rape is a difficult subject. How do you respond to someone who has just been raped? A wide range of emotions such as disgust, anger, self-blame, hurt, confusion and fear of it happening again. will be going through the mind of the victim.
Ensure they are in a safe place and encourage him/her to report what has happened immediately, especially before they have a shower, however repugnant that may seem. As with most things, prevention is better than cure, and sharing these tips may help prevent a traumatic experience from occurring, as well as the stress of the aftermath. If the rape was carried out by someone the" victim" knows, they

may be more reluctant to disclose information and may be worried about the consequences.

Madeleine Black – The Courage Cultivator is an international speaker, podcaster and author. I heard her story at an event, and I have read her book – Unbroken. It is a story about innocence, vulnerability and incredible personal strength. The story of her rape at 13 and how it affected and shaped her life is worth a read. She is also a successful podcaster, also called Unbroken.

www.madeleineblack.co.uk/unbroken-the-podcast-with-madeleine-black

---

PROTECTION TIPS

- **Always** *have your phone fully charged*
- **Carry** *a personal alarm or spray*
- **Avoid** *secluded places with new people*
- **Don't** *stay with anyone who makes you feel uncomfortable*
- **Trust** *your instincts and remove yourself from situations that don't feel right*
- **Watch** *out for spiked drinks*
- **Inform** *friends if you go off with someone*
- **Always** *call for help if needed*
- **Learn** *some basic self defence*

STAY SAFE

BEREAVEMENT
100,000+ deaths due to Coronavirus, means 100,000+ families are grieving. Trying to cope with grief and

arranging funerals for a totally unexpected loss can be heart breaking as well as stressful.

The distress of not being by a loved one's bedside in their final hours is hard to imagine, but that was the reality for so many.

Usually our first experience of loss is that of a grandparent or pet, which can cause both emotional pain and confusion. It's hard to comprehend what is going on, and grieving parents do not always realise that their children do not understand and feel lost, sometimes abandoned, and rejected, and some blame themselves for what has happened.

I can recall that my parents did not allow me, at the age of nine, to go to my grandmother's funeral. I felt cheated of not being able to say goodbye. Of course, I had no idea how traumatic it might have been, but it also might have prepared me for later loss. Unbelievably, my aunt (my mother's sister) and my paternal grandmother died on the same day when I was a student at nineteen. My dad rang to tell me, and I just couldn't absorb it. I felt very alone, and it was a few days before I could be with my family.

I went to two funerals in three days – one cremation and one burial. I found it awfully hard and didn't know which parent to comfort!

There is no doubt that most parents do what they believe to be right at the time, and it's a tough call. Sharing grief, however, can start the healing process, and helps us to realise that we are not alone with our feelings.

Loss and separation are obviously not just about death, but the effect can be almost as devastating.

Zoe's behaviour had changed dramatically over a few months. She was angry and irritable, not coping at school and altogether acting out of character. It transpired that her gran had died in year six, she went to a new high school where none of her old friends went, her cousins moved away, and her cat died. She felt hurt, bewildered, and confused. She didn't understand how the accumulated loss had affected her. Once she managed to join up the dots and understand what was happening and why she felt the way she did, she was able to cope and release the hurt and feelings of rejection with EFT, and she settled down.

Grief is one of the most painful emotions that we can experience but we need to go through it to come out on the other side and resume a new normality.

Historically, grieving was expected and accepted as being a twelve-month healing process but during the first world war, women were not allowed to have time to grieve as they were needed to keep industries and the war effort going. Bereavement "leave" was reduced to two weeks but it is impossible to heal in such a short period.

Loss of a Partner / Close Friend / Loved One

Losing someone you love, at any age is a major cause of stress. It is not something we expect to experience as a student, but the pandemic has changed that and most of us know of someone who has lost a loved one.

Statistics (ONS) show that over the last twenty years, the main causes of student deaths are accidents, suicides and interestingly, poisoning.

Death is more likely amongst your parents and grandparent's generation, in the natural order of life. Keep an eye on them because when we get older, we become more vulnerable and struggle more to cope with loss. Loneliness is a key factor in triggering depression after the death of a spouse. The stress of dealing with a terminal illness and indeed, sudden death, takes its toll and weakens the immune system. This in turn makes us susceptible to germs and illness.

If you are grieving, sleep may seem impossible, but it is important in the recovery process. Your GP can advise on mild medication for a short time or relaxation audios can help as well.

There is no right or wrong way to feel – shock, relief, guilt, anger, blame, exhaustion, and fear are all common and natural responses.

Emotional pain drains our inner resources and life feels pointless. No matter what anyone says it is a process which we must find our own way through until we can recover and experience life in a different way.

The one certainty that we all have in this life is death, but we are never prepared for it or know how to cope with it. Friends and family don't really know what to say or do to help or comfort you. They may be embarrassed by your tears or know instinctively to hug and hold you. Tell them what you are feeling and what you need most – to be left alone, to have meals prepared, to talk and miriness or even help with funeral arrangements or probate.

If you do lose someone you love, your university will probably have a compassionate leave allocation and procedure.

The days following a demise are usually busy with people around, it is after things have died down that the real grieving starts. Lockdown of course has denied friends and families the opportunity to support and assist with funerals and wakes. Feelings of guilt and letting people down has become prevalent, our traditional rituals have been destroyed making it a heavy burden to deal with alone.

Writing an emotional journal can help, as can seeing a therapist or someone from your religious community or church. GP's can offer information on local bereavement support groups.

Ann lost her husband to cancer. Although it was expected after a long illness, it was still hard to accept. She had two daughters, both of whom had weddings pending soon after their father's death. Wedding planning, probate, and sorting things out for her husband's business took up Ann's time. She trained for a new career and then suddenly without warning, she felt that her life had fallen apart. She became depressed, she wasn't sleeping or eating properly, she became a recluse and wanted to hide away. The tipping point came when her manager on a work placement was overly critical of her efforts.

She realised that she needed to do something about it but hadn't related her low self-esteem to her grief. She felt that she should be able to cope after a period had lapsed.

There is no time limit – we all grieve in different ways, but the process of grieving is especially important and usually follows the pattern on the diagram. Some emotions are not experienced in the same order but that is natural as we are all different.

Whatever the loss, it is perhaps reassuring to know that we go through a process and this can take longer for some than others. We need to consider being kinder to ourselves and not allowing anything to interfere with our grief.

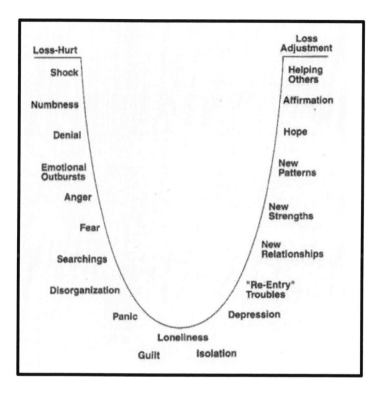

BONUS OFFER
Loss audio **www.stressworxbooks.com**
www.cruse.org.uk

DISABILITY
Disabilities are defined collectively under the Equality Act 2019
"Physical or mental impairment that has a substantial and long-term adverse effect on your ability to carry out normal day -to - day activities"

A more useful understanding is:
- Physical impairment.
- Sensory impairment.
- Learning impairment.
- Mental illness

- Various types of chronic disease
- Hidden disabilities

Having a disability from birth is quite different from having to adjust to changed circumstances after an accident or illness. We hear of amazing stories of people like Douglas Bader who flew in the war with artificial legs and Oscar Pistorius and other Paralympians who achieve incredible things without limbs. They are an inspiration, but maybe seem unreal to a person stuck at home without support networks. Social isolation is a major problem for many disabled people which can affect their mental health and wellbeing.

It is obvious when someone is in a wheelchair to assume that they may need some assistance, but few people really try to understand how that person may be feeling. Able bodied people tend to patronise wheelchair users and talk over them to a carer or ignore them all together.
Imagine how that feels......

Having been deaf from an early age, I have had no choice but to accept it. I see many older people who have age related hearing loss who find it hard to accept and become terribly upset, stressed, frustrated and angry with themselves and the people around them. They become stubborn and refuse to accept that hearing aids will relieve that stress!

Hidden disabilities are sometimes the hardest to live with. Someone may be struggling with arthritis, fibromyalgia, epilepsy, a heart condition, or chronic fatigue, none of which are obvious as the sufferers do not have a stick or wheelchair to make a public statement. How many times have you rushed past someone who is going up stairs slowly at a station or is getting in your way in a busy high street? Do we stop and think that they may be struggling or just curse and rush on past? If it were a mother with a buggy, would your response be different? We are particularly good at making assumptions about other people's behaviour without considering alternative reasons for it.

My mother had polio as a child which left her with one leg shorter than the other and one foot was size 6 and the other size 3. She had to but two pairs of shoes and throw the spare ones away.

She was a medical secretary at our local hospital which was the "home" hospital for a polio specialist. I used to go and sit with girls (boys didn't seem to so be affected) who were in "iron lungs" and chat or read to them. I can recall a few occasions when my mum and I would push the iron lung with a young person inside to our house, which would take about half an hour. It must have been at the weekend because my dad would take off the front door so that we could get the iron lung into the hallway so that the girl could watch TV. We would then have to push it back again and it was hard work!

Thankfully, polio is one of the diseases that has been controlled by vaccinations. I always felt that I was lucky to have full mobility.

How would you measure your disability awareness on a scale of 1-10?

www.disabilityrightsuk.org

DISCRIMINATION
"The unjust or prejudicial treatment of different categories of people, especially on the grounds of race, age, disability or sex."

The Equality Act 2010 defined the protected characteristics. This means that it is illegal to discriminate against the following due to:
• Age
• Disability (including mental illness)
• Gender Reassignment

- Marriage & Civil Partnership
- Pregnancy & Maternity
- Race
- Religion or Belief
- Sex

All universities are required by law to take action to protect their employees and students from direct discrimination, indirect discrimination, discrimination arising from a disability, harassment, and victimisation. They must also make reasonable adjustments to ensure that the facilities are fully accessible in terms of whatever is needed.

Being discriminated against, for whatever reason, can be hurtful and demoralising and is abhorrent. The support for Black Lives Matter has been quite incredible following the death of George Floyd.

Every UK university has a complaints procedure and policy when it comes to discrimination.

If you are facing discrimination from other students or staff at your uni because of your faith, culture, nationality, disability or sexuality, how can you stop it?

What to look for:
- Cultural slurs
- Using offensive and derogatory language
- Physical aggression and violence
- Exclusion
- Insensitive jokes

Discrimination from another student
- If you feel that it's safe to do so, tell the individual(s) concerned that they are offending you (if it's verbal abuse)
- Tell them you will take it further if it doesn't stop
- Report it to a tutor the university security

- If you feel you are in immediate danger, call 999 and ask for the police (physical abuse)
- Make a formal or informal complaint via your course leader, student services, the students' union who will help you resolve the matter

Discrimination from a member of staff

It may feel easier to tackle discrimination from a fellow student than a faculty member. They should definitely know better and have no excuse for their behaviour. Seek support from Student Services or the NUS to make a formal complaint using the complaints procedure.

You may be able to make your complaint anonymously or you may prefer to "go public".

The Government Equalities Office offers guidance on helping students decide if they have a valid complaint and how to approach and question their education provider.
The next step to take if you are not satisfied with the way your complaint is dealt with, you can take it to the Office of the Independent Adjudicator for Higher Education. This is an independent body set up to review student complaints in England and Wales for free.

Students in Northern Ireland can contact the Office of Northern Ireland Ombudsman and those in Scotland can contact the Scottish Public Services Ombudsman.
Even if you are not sure if it is actually   discrimination or not, keep a record of events, comments etc. for about a month or so. (you may also be able to get witness statements if others saw what happened) Talk to someone like your tutor, Student Union representative, or student counsellor to discuss your options.

They should be able to advise you but if the situation is not resolved then you can take the formal route. Each uni will have a complaints policy and procedure. Decide what outcome you are seeking:

- For action to be taken against the perpetrator (s) to stop the discrimination
- For the university to review a decision they've already taken
- Deadline extension for work submission
- A change in the university policy
- Compensation – for example, for stress or injury
- An apology
- For the student or staff member to be reprimanded or dismissed/ have their student status revoked

Your university is legally bound to protect you from discrimination under the Equality Act 2010. They cannot discriminate against you in relation to:
- Admissions
- How education is provided
- Exclusion
- Any other disadvantage, denial of opportunity or choice
- Teaching
- Assessments and exams
- Facilities, including lecture halls, libraries, and IT
- Leisure, recreation, entertainment, and sports facilities
- Physical environment, or
- Disciplinary procedures.

Each university/college is obligated by law to act if a student has experienced discrimination.

If you are a to witness discriminatory acts – what will you do? We all have a choice – to collude, ignore or act. Will you challenge the perpetrator there and then, make a note of what happened, or report it?

www.equalityhumanrights.com

I have never understood why Catch up TV does not have available subtitles, nor do I understand why films on planes don't either. To wear the headphones or ear buds supplied on planes, I must take my hearing aids out and the volume control is never adequate. Discrimination or a technical / cost issue?

TIPS TO CHALLENGE DISCRIMINATION

- **Think** about how you would feel if you were the victim – what help would you want/ need?

- **Intervene** as soon as possible (get someone else to be with you)

- **Ask** the perpetrator to stop, politely but firmly to show him/her that this behaviour is unacceptable.

- **Don't** provoke the perpetrator.

- **Stay** calm (even though it feels scary / challenging)

- **Record** the incident for evidence.

- **Reassure** the victim. Make eye contact and let them know that you are there to help.

- **Do not** put yourself at risk. If you are alone and things escalate, call the police.

- **Don't** use discriminatory language at any time

Some ago, I was at Waterloo station quite late on a Sunday evening. Suddenly there was siren going off and a disembodied voice saying something that I could not follow. If I had been on my own, I would not have had a clue what was going on – no visuals to be seen. Surely with all the video screens available in the station, one could have been utilised to supply information. Apparently, it was a routine fire drill.

I can feel a new challenge coming on...

BULLYING AND HARASSMENT

Any form of bullying or harassment is hurtful, upsetting, and stressful. Cyberbullying makes it easy for the bully to perpetuate his/her behaviour 24/7. A bully intimidates, undermines, and tries to control the victim by any means possible. It is a power game where the bully humiliates, degrades, and offends for no obvious reason. It can cause distress, loss of self-confidence and self-esteem, isolation, fear, anger, withdrawal, anxiety, despair, and poor concentration which can lead to insecurity, illness, and even suicide.

Bullies are into power games – their words and actions make them feel powerful at the expense of the victim.
They use any excuse – size, weight, skin colour, behaviours, religion, or maybe no real reason at all. A bully will always find something!

I have seen people in their forties and fifties who were bullied at school or university and it has continued to affect their lives. The most important thing to remember about bullying is that it's the bully who has the problem, not the victim.

There is usually a need within the bully that prompts them to behave the way they do.
- They may think that bullying someone will give them some status or kudos.
- They might be feeling intimidated or threatened by the victim's ability which they do not have
- They may have been bullied themselves and do not know how to behave any differently.
- Their victim may remind them of someone who upset them or made them angry.
- They might be enjoying the attention or reaction.
- They might be having problems at home, so they are taking this out on someone else.
- They feel that bullying is the only way they can feel good and powerful inside.

- They might be finding it hard to cope and are taking their anger and frustration out on the victim.
- They might be bullying for a dare.

Constant bullying is very upsetting and stressful. It is usually very cleverly done too so it's hard to prove it is happening.

Bullying and harassment are covered by the Equality Act 2010. Bullying is not technically against the law, but harassment is.

Harassment is "unwanted conduct related to a relevant protected characteristic, which has the purpose or effect of violating an individual's dignity or creating an intimidating, hostile, degrading, humiliating or offensive environment for that individual". (Equality Act)

As with discrimination, there is no place for bullying or harassment on a university or college campus.

Harassment is "unwanted conduct related to a relevant protected characteristic, which has the purpose or effect of violating an individual's dignity or creating an intimidating, hostile, degrading, humiliating or offensive environment for that individual". (Equality Act)

As with discrimination, there is no place for bullying or harassment on a university or college campus.

A culture of bullying is not conducive to a happy and stress-free student life, so it is in the interests of the university / college to deal with it as soon as possible.

www.nationalbullyinghelpline.co.uk

TIPS to DEAL with
BULLYING and HARASSMENT

- **Check** *the uni Bullying Policy for guidance*

- **Try** *not to react or respond with anger or let the bully see you upset.*

- **Make** *sure you are not alone with the bully*

- **Ask** *any witnesses to record incidents*

- **Ignore** *nasty comments*

- **Accept** *that you are not the problem*

- **Challenge** *him/her if you can in front of witnesses*

- **Tell** *him/her to stop as it is a waste of their time and energy*

- **Keep** *a written record of anything that makes you feel uncomfortable*

- **Speak** *to your tutor or union rep.*

- **If** *informal approaches do not work - consider formal action*

CHOICES

Sometimes the challenges we face feel insurmountable leading to choices that have serious and long-term consequences. Our lives are defined by the choices we make – food, clothes, friends, courses, careers, health, behaviours, and partners. Sometimes these choices are instinctive and at other times, influenced by others, family friends, our cultures, and the media.

We all make mistakes along the way and it's easy to be wise with hindsight. Could the wrong choices be avoided, or do we have to learn the hard way and accept the consequences of those choices? How do you make decisions? Do you take the easy option or seek a challenge?

As children, we accept the choices that adults around us make for us but as we grow, we start to make our own choices, based on the information we have at the time. If this is your first year at uni – you may find you have lots of new choices to make. Don't stress if you make mistakes!

We are free to choose but we are not free from the consequences of our choices."
Steven Covey

SELF-HARMING

Many people who are stressed, depressed, and struggling do not believe that anyone can help them or that anything can change. Self-harming is a desperate bid to get rid of negative emotions, memories and thoughts that just will not go away. The monkey on the shoulder is firmly in control and the physical pain seems to be more manageable than the emotional distress and acts as a distraction even though it is only short-term relief. Interestingly, the over forties are less inclined to self-harm.

Ways of self-harming include:
• Cutting - usually on the arms or other places of the body which can be covered up
• Eating disorders – bulimia / - anorexia
• Excessive drinking
• Burning the skin
• Inserting objects into the body
• Hitting or bruising with objects
• Drug misuse and overdosing
• Exercising excessively

Whilst self-harming may offer some release from emotional pain, it is often followed by feelings of shame and guilt, which adds to the original problem. Many self-harmers keep it a secret as it's a very private and personal way of trying to deal with things. Sadly, it becomes a habit, and it becomes harder and harder to tell someone and find help for the original issue.

Most parents or family members are horrified and saddened if and when they discover that their loved ones are self-harming, and they feel helpless, often blaming themselves.

SUICIDE

When self-harming doesn't relieve the emotional pain and distress, and self-esteem and self-respect are at an all-time low, then suicide may seem like the only answer. People who commit suicide generally believe that the world would be a better place without them, that they are beyond help, and they are past caring how their loved ones would feel. Suicide is a choice that some people make, but it is not a rational choice, as the decision is usually made when desperation and loneliness dominate the mind.

Angie was seventeen and she was struggling with attendance at college. The work was manageable, but it was social anxiety that was the problem. It had been as issue for a while and she had dropped out of another college where her "friends" had rejected her for being miserable all the time. Her self-esteem was so low that she couldn't believe that anyone would want to be her friend or spend time with her. Her boyfriend dumped her and that was the final straw – she felt totally worthless, isolated and alone. She took an overdose. Fortunately, her parents found her, and she was ok. She started a new college, but the problem was still there.

We quickly identified when and where this started. It was in year seven when she didn't know anyone in her new high school class. She lacked confidence to reach out to others because they all knew each other from primary school. The pattern became established.

EFT quickly cleared the painful memories and then we worked on her fears and negative beliefs, followed by some self-esteem and confidence building.

After three sessions, she was back in college, a bit hesitant but determined to make friends and complete her course.
If you are determined to end your life, then nothing will stop you. However, if you have doubts, these tips may help but please give a thought to those you leave behind.

www.save.org
www.samaritans.org

TIPS FOR SUICIDAL THOUGHTS

- **Write** *down your negative feelings and thoughts*

- **On a good day** *write down what you are grateful for and look at it on a bad day.*

- **Don't** *be on your own - visit or ring someone*

- **Tomorrow** *is another day - you don't need to decide today*

- **Avoid** *your triggers - music, photos, films*

- **Avoid** *drugs and alcohol which affect your mood*

- **Try** *and distract yourself from the dialogue in your head - go for a walk, shop, go to the gym*

- **Share** *your thoughts and feelings with a friend*

- **Ring** *a helpline*

- **Have** *ICE (In Case of Emergency) numbers handy*

CHANGE

"It is not the strongest of the species that survive, nor the most intelligent, but the one most responsive to change."
Charles Darwin

Change was referred to briefly in **Stress Stuff** – do you react, respond or resist change?

Some changes in life are welcome and some are resisted. Reactions are different between choosing to change as opposed to enforced change. Working in local government meant being adaptable to change – change in politics, change in personalities, change in policies, change in budgets, it was never ending.

Changes in attitudes, beliefs and values are common during student years. Some embrace change with enthusiasm, others are wary and unsure. It tends to be a developmental process as we learn to make decisions and choices independently.

Enforced change however, (like the Manchester students being fenced in) can create ill-will and resentment as well as stress, misery, and worry.

Resistance to change:
- Fear of the Unknown
- Lack of information or misinformation
- Threat to skills, status, or power base
- No perceived benefits
- Low trust climate
- Poor relationships and communication
- Fear of failure
- Fear of looking ridiculous or stupid
- Culture bound
- Established norms which are averse to change
- Reluctance to let go of the "good old days"

(O'Connor 1998 adapted from Kubler-Ross 1969)

Change becomes stressful when there is lack of consultation and communication, and
- People planning comes last
- Communication doesn't win 'hearts and minds'
- Individual agendas are ignored
- Engagement isn't measured
- Mis-starts
- Making change an option
- Not involving those expected to implement the change
- Delegated to 'outsiders' to implement
- Decision makers don't 'walk the talk'

"Be the change you want to see in the world".
Gandhi

Most organisations, including universities need to change on a regular basis to keep up with trends, market forces and demands. *How* change is implemented is the key. When the consultations are inclusive and everyone is aware of proposed changes and the implications, there will be less stress around.

All universities have had to change their "modus operandi" this year. Some changes have been radical. Incremental and slow change is manageable whilst sudden, radical and major change is upsetting and unsettling and can lead to conflict.

Take a moment to consider how things have changed for you this year. Some of these changes may become permanent, others may not. Either way more change inevitably lies ahead.

As the Scouts say "Be prepared".

TIME

Making best use of your time at uni can be challenging. Are you making the most of your opportunities? Do you make the best use of your time or do you waste it? Is there a reasonable balance between studying and leisure time?

We all have 24 hours in every day, seven days a week for a total of 168 hours to accomplish what we need and want to do in our lives. Every day too, we let the time thieves steal time away from us. When the time thieves take control, we become stressed. This is applicable to our personal lives as well.

1. Poor planning. Students don't plan to fail but a lot of students fail to plan. Without a plan for each day we lose focus, procrastinate, and let the monkey on our shoulder dictate how we spend or waste our time.

2. Crisis management. Leaving things until the last-minute works for some people but for most of us, deadlines rob us of choice and the clock takes control, putting us under pressure

3. Procrastination. Putting that project, essay, thesis or dissertation off, or avoiding getting them done for no sound reason, creates stress. Brian Tracey "Eat that Frog" advises us to get the large tasks out of the way first then the others do not seem so intimidating. "First things First" is the third of the Seven Habits of Highly Successful people (see Helpful Stuff)

4. Interruptions. Unanticipated events, unexpected phone calls, messages, visitors or emails steal time away from your study. They are an integral part of life but how much time do they need or deserve? Do you deal with them immediately or decide when they deserve your time? Plan the time of day that works for you to return calls and respond to emails. Ask friends to come back later at a time that suits you.

5. Unnecessary meetings or lectures. Some meetings and lectures are unproductive and unnecessary, not best use of your time. – do you really need to go? Can your needs be met online? This decision will need to be made in future when "live" lectures resume.

6. Being disorganised Do you spend time shuffling through piles of paper trying to find the notes you need? De-stress by keeping your notes and files up to date so that your time is used efficiently.

7. Lack of information If you do not have the information you need to complete a task it can be frustrating and time wasting. Pre-order books and papers well in advance.

8. Poor technology. Not having the correct systems, software or apps can cause time loss. Losing the internet at a crucial time is stressful as well as time wasting.

The Time Quadrants

The time quadrants or matrix were the creation of Dwight Eisenhower, President of the United States from 1953 - 61. They were adopted and made popular by Steven Covey in his 7 Habits theory. It is a good model to understand how to manage time more effectively and avoid unnecessary stress.

A general guideline:
• If a task is urgent and important – action immediately
• If it is urgent but not important, action it soon but do not spend too long on it
• If it is important but not urgent, commit enough time to do it justice
• If it is neither important nor urgent, consider delegating it or dropping it until it moves into one of the other boxes

When planning a task, we usually allocate an amount of time for completion. If we complete within the allocated time slot, then we remain "in control". If, however we have lots of interruptions – we lose that control and are in "response" time. (= STRESS!)

Finding the balance between staying in control of our time and being available to meet the needs and demands of others is crucial to time management.
Another way of looking at it is the distinction between "Important and Urgent" tasks.

Important tasks are those that lead to an outcome and the urgent ones are those that present themselves with a short timescale for completion which puts you under pressure to complete. There is a constant pressure between Important and Urgent but good planning puts Important before Urgent because it keeps you in control!

Priorities should be assessed in terms of their importance, not their urgency.

	URGENT	NOT URGENT
IMPORTANT	**1. The Critical Zone** *always chasing your tail =* **stress and anxiety** **burnout** **weak performance**	**2. The Planning Zone** *in control of life* *balanced* *organised* **high performer**
NOT IMPORTANT	**3. The Action Zone** *minor routine tasks, need to be done but not moving you forward =* **feeling dissatisfied**	**4. The Ineffective Zone** *nothing else to do.* *paper pushing,* *procrastinating* **lack of responsibility**

Quadrant 2 is the least stressful

"To do" lists
A to do list is a standard tool in time management. It usually is a flat list of tasks that a person needs to complete. To increase the efficiency of the ordinary to do list, prioritise the tasks in four different categories:
1 - Important and urgent
2 - Important and not urgent
3 - Not important and urgent
4 - Not important and not urgent

Effective time management is learning say *no* to tasks in categories 3 and 4 to make more time for tasks in categories 1 and 2. Freeing yourself from doing the unimportant tasks leaves more time to focus on the important matters, stay in control and stress free.

A to do list also helps "The feel-good factor" when you tick off completed tasks. A simple pro forma can be used and updated each day. For example

Date	Task	1	2	3	4	Done!

PLANNING

"If you fail to plan, you plan to fail" .
Benjamin Franklin

Do you know what you are doing from day to day?
Planning is an important and practical tool which we can all use, wherever we are. Benjamin Franklin (US president) said "If you fail to plan, you plan to fail."

Of course, there are other sayings too, such as "The best-laid plans of mice and men often go awry," meaning that however well planned we are, sometimes things change. However, if we have a plan to start with then we can amend it as circumstances change.

The thought of planning can seem quite daunting, especially if we don't know where to start, but we make plans all the time. When we arrange social events, we plan where to meet, what we are going to do, how we are going to get there, who we are going with and so on. We plan our meals; holidays and what we are going to wear every day and these skills are transferable to all aspects of life.

Planning is a tool for getting ideas into action A plan helps organise the mind! It might seem a bit time-consuming at first, but it will save time and stress in the long run. Many people use the acronym SMART as a planning guide
Specific **M**easurable **A**chievable **R**ealistic **T**ime framed

Most plans "Begin with the end in Mind" Habit 2 of the 7 Habits. We have a goal or outcome to work towards. (Specific) We then need to break it down into small bite-size chunks to make it manageable.

WHAT, WHY, WHERE, WHEN, WHO and HOW are also useful hooks.

Sometimes, despite the best intentions and thorough planning, obstacles get in the way.
The main obstacles or hurdles are those within us – like fear of failure, fear of disapproval or rejection, lack of

confidence in our ability to succeed, frustration or lack of motivation.

It is extremely hard to remain motivated when you have no clear purpose for each day. It's easier to stay warm under the duvet and sleep but too much sleep can lead to lethargy. Set yourself some tasks each day to give yourself a reason to get up.

CONFLICT

Some form of conflict in relationships is almost inevitable. Conflict itself isn't a problem; how it's handled, however, can bring people together or tear them apart. Poor communication, disagreements and misunderstandings can be a source of anger and distance, or a springboard to a stronger relationship and happier future.

Different, beliefs, attitudes, values, living habits, personality clashes, rivalry and arguments can cause conflict, especially in halls and student houses. This can generate a tense and stressful atmosphere for all concerned.

In the workplace, there are procedures to deal with conflict but in a domestic situation – diplomacy, sensitivity and patience are probably your best bet!

TIPS TO RESOLVE CONFLICT

- **Discuss** *differences as they arise in a calm manner*
- **Don't** *leave it until you are ready to explode*
- **Try** *not to be defensive*
- **Listen** *to all points of view*
- **Accept** *responsibility where appropriate*
- **Say** *sorry if it's your fault! (This is a good tactic as it disarms the opposite argument)*
- **Accept** *that you may not always be right*
- **Don't** *let the situation get out of proportion*
- **Resist** *making assumptions*
- **Avoid** *badmouthing or backstabbing the other person – it will get back to them*
- **Deal** *with the issue – ignoring it will make it worse*
- **If** *you can't agree, find a compromise or mediator*
- **If** *it is unresolvable – move out*

7

HELPFUL

STUFF

Chapter 8 is devoted to EFT (Emotional Freedom Technique) which I think is an incredible self-help tool to release negative emotions, thoughts, and memories. There are obviously other ways too, which you may find helpful. Please note that I have not mentioned strategies that I have no training or personal experience of, but you may like to explore Body Talk, NLP, CBT, Havening, Light Therapy or whatever works best for you.

MANAGING YOUR STRESS

The ABC model to manage stress is easy to remember, easy to apply and applicable to any age and circumstance.

A = AWARENESS and ACTION - What causes you stress? How do you react? What can you do about it?

B = BALANCE and BREATHING – balance of body, mind and spirit. (Work, Rest and Play). Deep breathing slows the heart rate and increases the oxygen to the brain, so we think more clearly.

C = CHOICE, CHANGE and CONTROL - Choose to be proactive and change so you are in control of your thoughts, feelings, and actions.

Because stress is invisible – we often don't see it creeping up on us until we feel that we cannot cope, or it manifests itself physically.

Lockdown provided another dimension – studying with family either home working or on furlough, both of which may have caused stress and anxiety.

Stressed spelt backwards is *Desserts* but like many forms of "traditional "stress management, comfort eating doesn't provide any long-term benefit because it is not dealing with the root of the problem.

Having a Radox bath, a drink or a bar of chocolate may help short term, but they are not working on the subconscious mind.

Exercise releases the stress hormones which makes you feel better but if you are unhappy or worried when you start your exercise, you will be unhappy and worried when you finish.

RESILIENCE

Resilience is the ability to recover quickly from misfortune, illness or depression and adapt to adversity, trauma, tragedy, threats, stress and changing circumstances.

Look how quickly we all adapted to staying at home to prevent the spread of Covid 19. Resilience is not trying to bounce back as if nothing has happened or changed. "Ignore it and it will go away" is not true and does not work.

Good examples of people who are resilient are police officers, fire fighters, paramedics, doctors, nurses, and soldiers. They have had to adapt to be able to deal with the horrors that they can come across in their jobs. Resilience is important in surviving tough times.

An emotionally resilient person
• Demonstrates a genuine interest in what's going on around them.
• Solves problems effectively.
• Is assertive and capable of showing initiative.
• Shows empathy toward others.
• Is responsible and trustworthy.
• Sets and attains realistic goals or targets.
• Maintains a sense of purpose and a positive outlook

- Has healthy self-esteem and self confidence
- Lets go of the past and focuses on the future

We have seen so many examples of resilience in the past few months together with courage and persistence in risking personal health and lives for others.
As children grow, they will develop a natural resilience which will last them into adulthood. If they are flexible, willing, and able to adapt to and accept change. They then will be able to respond to challenges and the curve balls that life can throw us without thinking or feeling that it's the end of the world.

Dr. Kevin Ginsburg, a paediatrician who specialises in Adolescent Medicine in Philadelphia, created the "7 C's of Resilience". Initially they were designed for children and young people, but they are applicable to us all.

Competence, confidence, connection, character, contribution, coping, and control. I would add an eighth and ninth – culture and communities which play an enormous part in shaping us as characters. If you have grown up in a culture or community of drugs and crime, then it's much harder to be resilient and I have nothing but admiration for those who rise above it and make something of their lives. It's much easier to go with the flow, whatever that is, it's the same with peer pressure, many succumb for what they perceive to be an easy life, regardless of the consequences.

People who are resilient recover more quickly from anxiety, stress, and depression. However, resilient, or not, understanding what the triggers are for the anxiety is half the battle. Even better, understanding what the root causes are helps to make the links or see the patterns from the past. In that way, the phrase "This too will pass" comes into its own and the resilient person will accept this. Of course, some issues are complex, and it takes a therapist to help unravel what's going on. Being more resilient can help prevent mental ill health from happening.

Research shows that resilience can be learned, but in my experience the negative baggage needs to be disposed of first. Negative memories, negative thoughts, negative beliefs, and negative feelings can prevent resilience developing.

Arguably, we can become too resilient and lose touch with our emotions and be unaware or unable to empathise with others. It is certainly not the exclusive solution to dealing with stressful or challenging situations in the workplace. Being decisive or assertive may be alternative skills to develop.

TIPS TO DEVELOP RESILIENCE

- **Jot** *down good things that happen each day to increase positivity*

- **Live** *in the moment*

- **Listen** *to your body*

- **Embrace** *change*

- **Write** *down your strengths and build on them*

- **Write** *down what you like about yourself*

- **Set** *yourself achievable goals*

- **If** *you are criticised - accept it if deserved and reject if not*

- **Stay** *calm*

- **Don't** *make a drama out of a crisis*

- **Try** *and see challenges as opportunities*

211

HYPNOSIS

Hypnosis is the oldest form of healing known to man and it works on the conscious mind to make changes that you want and need. Most of us have heard of hypnosis, and it usually conjures up images of stage hypnosis where volunteers do daft things in response to directions from the hypnotist. What we are not told is that these 'volunteers' decided that they wanted to make fools of themselves before the show began, and probably had a practice session as well!

Let me assure you that if these characters did not _want_ to make fools of themselves under hypnosis, then they would come out of it immediately.

All hypnosis is self-hypnosis, and you may be surprised to know that we all enter degrees of hypnosis every day! How many times have you been daydreaming, and you suddenly realise that someone is talking to you? Maybe you are so involved in a film or a book that you miss being told that your meal is ready? Another good example is driving on the motorway and you reach your turnoff much more quickly than expected – you were in light hypnosis.

A hypnotherapist is merely the guide who directs and leads the person into the hypnotic state. It feels great, rather like that nice feeling when you are dozing on the settee and you are vaguely aware that the TV is on or someone is talking but you really can't be bothered to listen fully.

The therapist induces the hypnotic trance by using certain words and phrases which are directed at the subconscious mind and the conscious soon gets bored and drifts off – just like when you are drifting off to sleep. You are not fully awake, but neither are you completely asleep.

Another way to relax is to make your eyes tired by looking at a picture like this

Generally, most people remember either some or most of the experience. Suggestions which have been given in hypnosis become absorbed to produce changes in behaviour, beliefs, attitudes, values and feelings. The therapist will be aware of your issues and will be basically telling the subconscious that the fears, anxiety, painful memories, panic attacks etc are no longer needed. They may have served a purpose in the past but now is the time to release them and let them go. The role of the subconscious is to protect us so it will acknowledge and make changes that are for your benefit. In the same way, it will alert you to danger; if, for example, there was a fire, you would come out of hypnosis immediately.

Remember that you are always in control, and you will not say or do anything at all that you don't want to. If you were to be given suggestions that you didn't morally agree with you would come out of hypnosis immediately. The example I usually share with clients is that if I asked them (in hypnosis) to take their clothes off and run down the road, they would come out of hypnosis immediately unless they *wanted* to take their clothes off and run down the road!

Most people are aware of changes and feel different immediately after the session. Everyone is surprised when they look at the clock and see how long they were in hypnosis as it often just feels like five minutes when it was really half an hour.

No one can hypnotise you if you don't want to be hypnotised. Your natural defences will prevent this from happening. A hypnotherapist **CANNOT** (and **WILL NOT**) encourage you do anything against your will, morals, values or ethics. Hypnosis is not appropriate for anyone with a diagnosed mental illness like schizophrenia or those with special needs, who require personal attention. Hypnotherapy is not suitable for those who have ever suffered from personality disorders, psychosis, clinical depression or epilepsy.

However, hypnosis is **not** dangerous. It is just a natural state of the mind which is guided by the hypnotherapist as a means to help the individual change certain habits or patterns of behaviour and release painful memories. Your mind rejects any undesired or unwanted suggestions automatically.

Hypnosis is good for most causes of stress. It was recognised by the British Medical Association in the 1950's and is used by some doctors and dentists too. Some people have teeth extracted and others surgery whilst in hypnosis. Hypnobirthing has become very popular too.

Young adults are fascinated by hypnosis and embrace it whole heartedly. For children, metaphor is used, disguised as a bedtime story which can be listened to as an audio time and time again.

SELF HYPNOSIS

If you like the sound of your own voice, record the following stress relief script onto your phone so you can listen whenever you need to. Speak slowly and clearly. Alternatively, ask a friend to record it for you.

214

Take a nice couple of deep breaths and settle down in the chair. Close your eyes and allow yourself to start to relax and just let go of those everyday thoughts, stresses, and strains.

Now make yourself really comfortable and relax your body. I am going to ask you to imagine certain things, and you'll find that as you see the scenes I describe, the more relaxed and comfortable you become. See yourself walking along a secluded beach with white sand as far as the eye can see. The waves are gently lapping on the shore and the sound soothes you as you walk along the water's edge, The water is cool as it caresses and tickles your toes and you can feel your body slowing down as you start to relax. The sun is shining and it's the temperature that you like, and the soft sea breeze clears your mind of tension and stress, anxiety and worries, negative or painful memories, negative beliefs – anything and everything that is stopping you from feeling the best you can possibly feel...

With each and every breath that you take, you find yourself becoming more and more relaxed and comfortable. You see a couple of palm trees ahead with a hammock swinging between them. It looks inviting, so you stroll over to it and lie on the hammock. It sways gently in the breeze and you decide to rest a while. You stroll over to the hammock and lie down. The hammock sways gently and you find yourself drifting and floating.

You become aware of the sunlight above your head and you can feel the healing sunlight, warm and relaxing as it flows down you face and neck. Now feel that healing sunlight flowing across your shoulders and down your arms to the tips of your fingers. Become aware of your body slowing down as the sunlight surround your heart like a blanket of love. Your heart beats slowly, steadily and easily. The sunlight flows round your ribs and up your spine, soothing, calming, relaxing, releasing tension and stress. Now feel this healing sunlight entering your stomach, soothing, calming relaxing, releasing. Sense the healing light carrying on down your legs to the tips of your toes. Soothing, calming and healing, bringing your body into a healthy balance as it releases any tension, sadness., fears and anxiety, releasing any blockages, You feel as though you are becoming immersed in an ocean of calmness - an ocean of calmness, that continues, as peace and serenity take over your entire body, and your mind - creating within you a very special feeling inside .You become aware of the inner you which is calm and relaxed, clever and wise - the part of you that wants you to heal and to recover and become a whole person once more, free of stress and tension.

Feel the healing sunlight, sense it, imagine it filling every nerve every cell, each muscle, just feel it at work, soothing, calming, healing, relaxing and reenergising. This healing gentle sunlight is absorbing and destroying any reasons, causes and memories that have caused this stress and tension,– anything and everything that has contributed to your present situation, and no matter how long ago this started it is time to change. The more you listen to this audio, the more you will release. Just let the sunlight do its work, then see yourself wandering back to the hard, damp sand and picking up a stick, you write in the sand – whatever or whoever caused your stress. When you have written all you need to, watch the waves wash the words away.

Continue to relax now and then when you are ready, just drift back into this time and this place.........
You can amend accordingly – for exam or interview nerves etc.

EMDR
This is another therapy that I teach my clients as a self-help tool. Think back to **Mind Stuff** with the FedEx logo and I asked if you could see the arrow. Our eyes are especially important in terms of getting messages to the brain and

also indicating genuineness when making eye contact with others.

I am not getting into the argument about which way our eyes move when we are remembering or constructing things (lying) The original theories around this seem to have been disproved recently.

EMDR stands for Eye Movement Desensitisation Reprocessing and it has been around since. 1989 when it was discovered and developed by Francine Shapiro.

The therapist doe does not need to know all the detail of the event or emotion that needs to be cleared but a measurement is taken on a scale of 1-10 with 10 being high.

The therapist then moves his or her finger in a horizontal motion about a 3ft or metre distance. This is done 24 times after which the intensity of the memory or emotion drops.

Doing this yourself is easy too. You are not going to follow your own finger, but you can use a door, window or wide screen to follow from side to side. Your eyes become tired and you can feel your body slowing down.

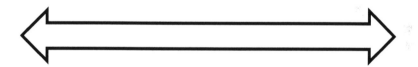

1. Follow the line there and back x 24 with your eyes, keeping your head still.
2. Take a deep breath in and out
3. Measure the intensity once more
4. If it has dropped so that it doesn't bother you any more then stop. If something else comes to mind…
5. Repeat

OR Change Direction
1. 24 eye movements again diagonally
2. Deep breath
3. Measure once more
4. 24 again on the opposite diagonal

Usually horizontal eye movements are sufficient to make an emotional shift.

It is a good way of getting off to sleep as he eyes tire quite quickly. Follow the top of a window or door with your eyes.

REIKI
I trained in Reiki to Advanced level but as I didn't have space for a bed in my therapy room, I decided to focus on EFT and hypnosis to build my practice. However, Reiki still fascinates me, and I love receiving it. It is a healing process which affects body mind and spirit. It is hard to describe the sensations of peace and tranquillity flowing through your body and mind. When you train in Reiki – Level One can be used for self-healing and relaxation. You are "attuned" by a Reiki Master and then when you deliver Reiki your hands feel warm and tingly and often the receiver can feel the heat. Reiki goes where it is needed to heal or relax.

REFLEXOLOGY
I really missed my monthly reflexology treatment during lockdown, I find it very relaxing and am always fascinated by what my therapist can detect from my feet! As with Reiki, Reflexology clears blocked energy by massaging pressure points on the feet and sometimes hands. You can Google pictures of the points and see how they correspond to different parts of the body.
The benefits of Reflexology include:
• Cleansing the body of toxins
• Boosting the immune system
• Increasing circulation
• Promoting healing
• Balancing energy

DEEP BREATHING
Breathing is a natural human function, and we need to breathe to live. However, stress or shock can lead to shallow breathing as we prepare for Fight or Flight.

Continuous shallow breathing then causes the body to stay in a stressed and tense state.
The more stressed we are, the shallower our breathing is likely to be.

Shallow breathing limits the amount of oxygen available to the body, causing the whole system to work less efficiently, and is a great contributor to the tiredness that so often results from stress. Bad breathing also restricts the blood flow to the brain, which can cause dizziness and tingling.
Low carbon dioxide levels put the body on high alert, which is exhausting.

Breathing exercise

Take a deep breath in through your nose and feel your stomach expanding. Count slowly to four and then breathe out, letting your stomach deflate, counting slowly to four once more. Be aware of the air entering and leaving your lungs. Aim for 8-10 breaths a minute. This will calm down the body and address the chemical imbalance of the stress hormones. Practice until you feel in control of your breathing and this then becomes your new habit.

MEDITATION

Meditation is a natural development from breath work. It can

- Lower blood pressure
- Improve blood circulation
- Lower heart rate
- Lessen perspiration
- Slow respiratory rate
- Reduce anxiety
- Lower blood cortisol levels
- Increase sense of well-being
- Lessen stress
- Deepen relaxation

SIMPLE MEDITATION

- Sit or lie comfortably
- Close your eyes
- Simply breathe naturally
- Focus your attention on your breath and how your body moves with each inhalation and exhalation
- If your mind wanders, bring it back to your breath

Practice for two to three minutes to start, and then for longer periods. This can be done quite easily and quickly to relax.

MINDFULNESS

Whilst meditation is emptying the mind to relax, mindfulness is being aware of all your senses and thoughts without being judgemental about them. There are apps available to guide you.

Yoga combines physical exercise with breathing and relaxation.

PHYSICAL EXERCISE

Physical exercise releases the cortisol and adrenalin that builds in our bodies when we are stressed. Any form of exercise is good, from walking to a whole range of sports activities.

The best exercise you can do is something that you enjoy, so you can keep fit, de-stress and have fun as well.
A good stretch works wonders.

AROMATHERAPY
Aromatherapy works through the sense of smell and skin absorption using a range of essential oils, many of which are blended together to enhance the benefits.
These oils are used to:
• manage pain
• improve sleep quality
• reduce stress and anxiety
• soothe sore joints
• treat headaches and migraines
• alleviate side effects of chemotherapy
• ease discomforts of labour
• fight bacteria, virus, or fungus
• improve digestion
• improve hospice and palliative care
• boost immunity

There is a wide range of oils and an equal number of providers and uses. Some say you can ingest some oils; others say not. The National Association for Holistic Aromatherapy provides information and details of accredited therapists **www.ifparoma.org**
Some oils have side effects so do check information carefully before use.

COLOUR THERAPY

There are some amazing colouring books that you can buy for little outlay. They are relaxing, and you also get a sense of achievement when you have completed one.

SMILE!

When you smile, the muscles that you use trigger the release of endorphins which are known as the "happy hormones". They not only make you feel better but also reduce the stress hormone cortisol. A fake smile works too! Remember that the mind doesn't know the difference between what is real and what is imagined.

Smiling is contagious and makes us more approachable as well as making others feel better too. Laughter too is a great stress reliever; think about how you feel after a good laugh... Laughter therapists tell you to fake it until you make it – a false laugh can still release endorphins and you cannot be stressed when you are laughing. Watch comedy shows, listen to comedians, have a giggle with friends, or spend time with children. (They laugh more than adults) laughter is infectious and we all feel better after a good laugh.

KEEP A JOURNAL

This is another easy way to offload feelings – a day to day diary, shop bought journal or plain notebook all offer a means of offloading thoughts and feelings each night.
Nobody else needs to see it but you will feel a bit calmer when you have put those thoughts and feelings onto paper. You will probably sleep better too.

ASSERTION

Being assertive is a great skill or strength to have.
Assertiveness means being able to express your needs, preferences and feelings in a way that is neither threatening or punishing to others, without stress, fear or anxiety, and without violating the rights of others.
It is a means of direct, honest communication between

individuals interacting equally and taking responsibility for themselves.

Non-assertiveness means:
* Having difficulty standing up for yourself
* Voluntarily relinquishing responsibility for yourself
* Inviting persecution by assuming the role of victim

ATTITUDE OF GRATITUDE
What are you grateful for in your life? Your warm bed? Food? Friends? Partner? Family? Health? Warm clothes? Sunshine? The birds singing. flowers? Your phone, pet, music? Write your own list and when you have a bad day, look at it and think of people who have none of these things, however simple they may seem. You will feel a bit better and this helps to get things into perspective.

The 7 Habits of Highly Effective People

I trained as a Master Facilitator for the 7 Habits Teen programme which Sean Covey adapted from the original, written by his father. It is a useful model for planning which reduces stress.

THE HABITS

1. **Be proactive** - *This is the ability to take responsibility and control of life – rather than letting anyone else do so.*

2. **Begin with the end in mind** – *What and where is your destination? Once that is decided, a route can be planned.*

3. **Put first things first** - Having worked out a destination the first steps can be taken to work towards identified goals.

4. **Think win-win** - Win-win is based on fairness and not trying to succeed at the expense of anyone else.

5. **Seek first to understand and then be understood.** – watching, listening, and learning from others helps to understand where they are coming from and be a much better communicator than otherwise.

6. **Synergise** – *"The whole is greater than the parts"- working with others can be more positive and productive than working in isolation.*

7. **Sharpen the saw** – *a strange phrase which is about balance and self-renewal – meeting emotional, physical, spiritual, and social needs as well as intellectual. This means regular breaks, exercise, and fun!*

Think of the opposite – not planning, being unfair, not listening or working with others, being lazy and not taking any exercise. Which sounds better?

8

TAPPING STUFF

Introduction to Emotional Freedom Technique

EFT is one of the best ways I have found to take control of negative emotions. I am still amazed by the results after eighteen years of using it. It is better known as "tapping" because we use our fingertips to tap on meridian points to free up physical discomfort, painful memories, and negative emotions. It is based on the principles of acupuncture but there are no needles!

EFT, otherwise known as Emotional Freedom Technique, combines ancient Chinese acupressure and modern psychology with incredibly quick, powerful, and long-lasting results. **Tapping can help** with pain relief, healing past traumas and painful memories, clearing limiting or negative beliefs, emotional eating and drinking, weight loss, food cravings, fears and phobias, negative thinking patterns and habits.

The EFT journey began in the 1970's quite by chance and is now used all over the world.

Dr. Roger Callahan, a clinical psychologist in the US, was looking for ways to help his clients eliminate fears, phobias, habits and painful memories. He was interested in how acupuncturists used the meridians to help relieve pain.

If you have ever been to an acupuncturist, you may recall posters on the wall showing the meridian system. They look like lines running throughout our bodies from top to toe. Take a moment to Google body meridians in Images and you will see what I mean.

Reflexologists massage the meridian points in your feet which are all connected to the major organs of the body. The meridians carry our energy round our bodies, just like veins and arteries carry blood. By tapping on identified places on the upper body and face, blockages can be cleared.

It sounds a bit bizarre, but it is the most powerful self-help technique I have come across. After all, we have our fingertips and feelings with us all the time, so we can deal with emotions as they arise.

Dr. Callahan was working with a woman called Mary who had an irrational fear of water. He had tried everything in his toolbox but as he was studying the meridians, he asked Mary where she felt the fear. She said it was in her stomach. The meridian point for the stomach is under the eye so she was asked to tap under her eye with her fingertips. This she did and her fear was released.

With this success, Roger Callahan went on to develop a series of sequences to use to different issues. This was known as TFT (Thought Field Therapy). However, it was rather complex and involved tapping all over the body by a practitioner.

He went on to train others, and one of his students in 1991 was a guy called Gary Craig who developed a simple and easy to remember sequence called EFT - Emotional Freedom Technique.

A calm mind creates a calm body and what the mind suppresses, the body expresses.

Think of being anxious before an exam – do you feel sick and shaky? The mind /body connection is invisible, but it is there, just like our meridians.

In the same way that our arteries and veins carry blood around our bodies, meridians carry our energy. If the flow of energy is blocked, then we experience physical discomforts and eventually disease.

So, what can cause a blockage? Negative emotions, negative memories, negative beliefs, and thoughts – in other words – STRESS!

EFT has grown rapidly in the USA since its creation and it is used with soldiers and others suffering from post-traumatic stress from 9/11 and other traumatic events in peoples' lives with amazing results.

By tapping on meridian points – you can clear your baggage quickly and easily. If you have had a bad day then a couple of rounds of tapping will help you feel relaxed and calm.

As I explained earlier in **Mind Stuff**, our minds are in two parts – the conscious and the subconscious. The amygdala is the part of the subconscious mind that acts as the gatekeeper, on the lookout for external threats. It alerts you by triggering the stress response as well as releasing cortisol and adrenaline which prepares the body for fight or flight.

When you are upset and stressed about anything, you can't think straight. EFT helps bring both parts of your mind onto an even keel as well as calming your body and the amygdala down. It's a win win all round.

As we now know, the subconscious mind is *immensely powerful*.

Try this….

Imagine a plank of wood lying across your hallway; if I asked you to walk along it, you would have no problem at all. If, however, I asked you to imagine this same plank of wood stretching across a crevice, one hundred feet up, I am sure that your reaction would be different! Although you know this isn't a REAL situation, your own experiences, memories and beliefs trigger your imagination and the emotion that caused distress, which in turn, in this instance, recreates fear, shortage of breath, shaking and so on. The negative emotion that is triggered by the memory or thought prevents energy flowing through certain meridians. Tapping on these meridians releases the negativity, neutralises the emotion, and stimulates the meridian energy points, which allows the physical symptoms to disappear.

*EFT cannot change what's happened, but it **DOES** change the way you feel about it.*

The sequence below is very general, but it will become more specific with examples later in this chapter.

First, you need what is called a "set up statement" where you acknowledge the problem. Let's use a fear of heights as an example.

Even though I am scared of heights

Now we choose a solution

I choose to release my fear

The original EFT "basic recipe" uses "I deeply and completely love and accept myself" but many people find that hard to say, especially at first because they don't love and accept themselves at all, and that's why they feel so bad! (The "Choices" method was developed by Dr Pat Carrington in 2000.)

By saying it out loud, both your conscious mind and subconscious mind are hearing the same thing at the same time – usually they are saying different things to you. Your subconscious is going round like a hamster on a wheel whilst your conscious is saying things like "pull yourself together "or "you're just being silly."

Now, how strong is that fear? How intense is it?
Can you measure it on a scale of 1-10 with 10 being the highest?

Now we say our statement out loud three times whilst we tap on the "Karate Chop" point on our hand. It doesn't matter which hand you use. Use all your fingers of one hand to tap on the other as in the diagram.

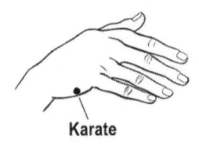

Karate

You may find that your hand tingles a bit when you have done this, but that's fine. The technical term for this is "psychological reversal" but simply put, it's making sure that your batteries are in the right way. (Think of a torch which won't work if the batteries are not put in correctly.)

Using two fingers, index, and middle finger, and say out loud as you tap on the following points *"This fear of heights".* You can use either hand on either side of your face.

Eyebrow - EB *At the beginning of the eyebrow, just above and to one side of the nose*

Side of Eye - SE *On the bone at the side of the eye, level with your eyeball*

Under Eye - UE *On the bone under an eye about 1 inch below your pupil*

Under Nose - UN Between *the bottom of your nose and the top of your upper lip*

Chin - Ch *Middle of your chin*

Collarbone - CB *To the right or left of where a man would tie his tie (trace your collar bone towards your throat until you find a knobbly bit – your clavicle)*

Under the Arm - UA *About 4 inches below the armpit.*

Top of Head - TH *Centre of scalp*

Take a deep breath in and out

Now we focus on the positive choice.

Go through the tapping points again but this time you say: *"I choose to release my fear"* or *"I'm cool"* or *"I accept myself anyway"*
- Eyebrow
- Side of Eye
- Under Eye
- Under Nose
- Chin
- Collar bone
- Under arm
- Top of Head

Take another deep breath (this shifts the energy and clears the emotion).

Now reassess your score – feel any better? Has the fear come down on your scale? Maybe it's harder to find? I am sure it does feel different! Follow the diagram on the next page.

However, there may be a reason for your fear, like a fall, so we need to work on the memory to clear the fear completely.

www.thetappingsolution.com

Before we do that, there is another short sequence that should help to reduce the fear a bit more.

It may seem a bit weird but go for it and I will explain afterwards.

It's called the Gamut and we start by tapping on the gamut point which is on the back of the hand between the ring finger and little finger.

Tap this point as you:

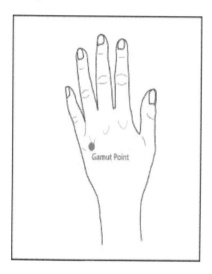

- Close your eyes
- Open your eyes
- Keep your head still and look hard down to the right
- Keep your head still and look hard down to the left
- Roll your eyes all the way round anti – clockwise
- Repeat clockwise
- Hum the first line of "Happy Birthday"
- Count from 1-5 aloud
- Hum "Happy Birthday" again
- Take a deep breath

Eye movement is very important in terms of messages to the brain. Happy Birthday usually triggers happy memories (but you can choose another tune if you wish). Memories and rhythm represent your subconscious and the 1-5 counting, represents your conscious, so it's like they are agreeing to work together. Somehow this procedure brings down the feeling even more!

I am not really sure how my car works but as long as it does, I don't worry.

233

Reassess your score once again. If it is now zero or a low number that feels comfortable then you can stop.

5 is obviously the halfway point – any emotion that is above 5 is in control of you. Below 5, then you have more control of the emotion. The lower you get it, the better.

If you need to reduce the issue even more then this time your statement will be
"Even though I have this remaining (fear of heights) I choose to let it go."

Continue to tap using the word "remaining."   "This remaining fear of heights…"

Whilst you are tapping, a new thought or a memory may pop into your head – this is part of the de-layering process which your subconscious is responding to as you tap and release those emotions.

Remember the filing cabinet I referred to in **Mind Stuff**? It is all in there. Keep a note of what comes up and then tap for that as well. You will be surprised at how much better you feel.

Whatever your fear the chances are that there is a reason for it. Maybe you had a bad experience or saw something on the TV or a film which has caused your fear.

Have a think.
"Even though I have this horrible memory of………." (be as specific as you can) I choose to let it go, I accept myself anyway."

There are loads of negative feelings, thoughts and memories that can hold you back. However, you do not have to go on living with them. By using EFT, you can neutralise negative thoughts and feelings, and even change them to positive ones. Awareness or identifying the feeling is the first step to change.

Think of an orange. When you remove the skin, there are lots of segments.

The peel holds them together, but which segment do you eat first? It's the same with tapping; you may start with one issue and that leads you to the next. They are all connected. Another way of looking at your issues is to imagine a jig saw puzzle where you need to find the missing pieces to complete the picture. These are called aspects in the EFT world.

Have a look at the common negative emotions below and identify the ones that resonate or mean something to you and work your way through them.

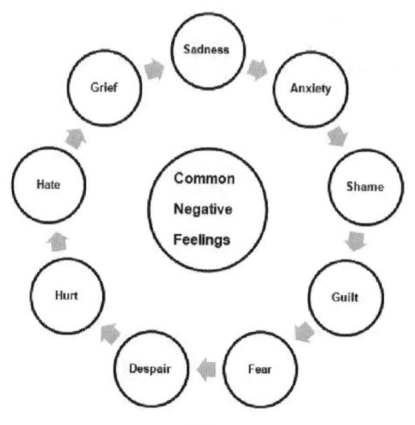

Take note of any memories that may emerge that have had an impact upon you. Work on those too. Every uncomfortable memory we have (as well as good ones) is stored in the subconscious. Subsequent events that are similar trigger the same emotions, so if you clear the original memory, the feelings will not come back.

This is known as the perfect peace procedure Write down every event or memory that has upset you, imagine it's a movie and give it a name, like "When I was teased about my jumper when I was 8." Measure its intensity and tap it out.

Even though I have this horrid memory of being teased when I was eight, I choose to let it go now.
Most problems or issues start somewhere so allow old memories to surface – there is almost inevitably a link between an old, stored memory and the feelings you are having now.

A memory is like a picture or a movie in your mind and the more you think about it, the stronger it gets. If a memory picture, song or movie cause upset then it needs to be cleared. Obviously, nothing can change what has actually happened, but we can change the intensity of the emotion which is linked to that memory.

We can give the picture or movie a name like "That horrible day" or break it down into "scenes" and work through them. You can work on it in two ways:

E.g. *Even though I have this hurtful memory of that horrible day*

Even though I feel angry with… When I think of that horrible day

I choose to release the memory, or I choose to let it go

Or - Just bring up the picture in your mind like a photo

Even though I have this horrible picture in my mind

Even though I can remember that horrible day clearly

I choose to let the picture fade, or I choose to let it go

Either way, you will find that the memory or picture recedes, and when you do the gamut as well it fades even more. It is comparable to the difference of seeing a film in black and white instead of colour. It loses its impact and fades into insignificance.

If something else comes into your mind as you are going through this process, tap for that next. It is your subconscious giving you a connection.

Remember that you can't change what has happened, but you can change how you feel about it!

Put a number beside the emotion and then create your statement. It is a good idea to write it down so that you can monitor your progress. Be as specific as you can. You can use the past or present tense, whichever is appropriate.

See the examples below and finish the sentences.
Even though **I worry** (insert what you worry about). I choose to release the feeling
Even though I am **impatient** when
Even though I **hate**
Even though I feel/felt I am not **good enough**
Even though I feel/felt **anxious** about
Even though I feel /felt **hurt** when
Even though I feel/felt **scared** of
Even though I feel / felt **desperate** when
Even though I feel /felt **angry** with (or when)
Even though I feel / felt **sad** when
Even though I feel / felt **lonely**

237

Even though I don't feel **loved**
Even though I feel /felt **rejected when**
Even though I feel / felt **ashamed**
Even though I feel / felt **hopeless**
Even though I feel / felt **miserable**
Even though I feel/felt **angry** with

You can also release stress and tension which is trapped in your body. Where do you feel it when you are nervous or anxious?

Even though my stomach is churning... I choose to relax and let go.

Even though my chest is tight and tense... I choose to release the feeling

Get rid of anything and everything holding you back. Clear all that unwanted and unneeded baggage!

You can use your other senses for tapping too. You might recall a smell or colour that is attached to the situation you are trying to clear.

For example. *Even though I can remember the smell in the old house, I choose to release it now.*
Even though I have this hot red anger inside, I choose to release it.

"The Tapping Solution" by Nick Ortner invites you to imagine a tree. The symptoms are the leaves, the branches are your emotions, the trunk represents events, and the roots are your limiting beliefs.

Your symptoms are where you feel the discomfort in your body
Even though: *My stomach is churning, I have a headache, I am irritable, edgy*

Going down the tree, after dealing with your emotions, events (memories) that caused the issue are next, followed by your limiting (negative) beliefs.

The following pages are to give you ideas of tapping sequences and statements for various issues that may be in your life.

EFT for STRESS / ANXIETY

Create a statement that describes how you feel (or work through all of them, one at a time). Look at the choices below and choose the best match or add your own.

Measure the intensity of the feeling on a scale of 1-10

Even though:

I feel stressed, overwhelmed, edgy, irritable, anxious about, I can't cope, I'm tearful, I feel defensive, I lack motivation, I've lost my mojo, I can't be bothered with anything, I forget things all the time, I can't switch off, I can't relax, my stomach is churning, I feel shaky, my throat / chest feels tight and tense....

I choose to:

❖ Be calm and relaxed
❖ Let it go
❖ Take back control
❖ Release the feeling
❖ Feel more energetic
❖ Remember important things
❖ Relax my body
❖ Clear my head

What is the intensity of the feeling now?

Do the Gamut. (see next page)

Tap for any memories or events which are contributing to or triggering your stress. When did you start to feel like this? What was going on your life?

Some practitioners have ceased using the Gamut but I find it useful and can reduce the intensity quite rapidly. Eye movement – as we saw with the FEDEX logo is important in terms of messages to the brain. This procedure involves eye movement plus a bit of rhythm and usually happy memories with Happy Birthday which represents the subconscious. The 1-5 count represents your conscious mind so the two are working together. You can of course choose another tune if birthdays were not happy occasions for you.

THE GAMUT

Tap between the valley or join of your ring finger and little finger

❖ Close your eyes
❖ Open your eyes
❖ Keep your head still and look hard down to the right
❖ Keep your head still and look hard down to the left
❖ Roll your eyes all the way round anti – clockwise
❖ Repeat clockwise
❖ Hum the first line of "Happy Birthday"
❖ Count from 1-5 aloud
❖ Hum "Happy Birthday" again
❖ Take a deep breath

Now reassess your score – don't forget to tap for anything else that comes into your mind. This is your subconscious telling you that there is a connection with the original issue.

EFT for NEGATIVE BELIEFS

Create a statement that describes your beliefs (or work through all of them, one at a time). Look at the choices below and choose the best match or add your own.

Measure the intensity of the feeling on a scale of 1-10

Start with your strongest negative beliefs.

Even though I believe..... (Whichever it is)

I am - useless, thick, fat, skinny, ugly, too short, too tall, unlovable, lazy, aggressive, a failure, no one loves or likes me, always late, not understood, I have no friends, a lousy friend, dishonest. I have no confidence, I can't trust anyone, No one trusts me, I'll never be happy, I always get hurt, I am guilty of.....

I choose to

❖ Change my belief
❖ Believe in myself
❖ Let it go
❖ Have faith in myself
❖ Trust myself
❖ Stay calm and relaxed
❖ Stop worrying
❖ Accept myself anyway
❖ Be calm and confident
❖ Feel in control

What is the intensity of the feeling now?
Do the Gamut

Tap for any memories that may be connected to these negative and limiting beliefs.

EFT for CHANGE

Create a statement that describes how you feel (or work through all of them, one at a time). Look at the choices below and choose the best match or add your own.

Measure the intensity of the feeling on a scale of 1-10

Even though

I am scared of change, I dislike change, I feel out of control, the change is too fast for me, I am confused with the changes, I am worried how the change will affect me

I choose to

- ❖ Accept what I cannot control
- ❖ Check I have all the information I need
- ❖ As for clarification
- ❖ Release my frustration
- ❖ Stop worrying
- ❖ Go with the flow
- ❖ Embrace the change
- ❖ Look for opportunities
- ❖ Move on if I cannot accept the change

What is the intensity of the feeling now?
Do the Gamut

Remember to tap for whatever may come into your mind as this will be connected to the issue. What changes have you dealt with in the past? Tap for uncomfortable memories relating to change.

EFT for BODY IMAGE

Create a statement that describes how you feel (or work through all of them, one at a time). Look at the choices below and choose the best match or add your own.

Measure the intensity of the feeling on a scale of 1-10

Even though

I dislike my body; I hate my arms, legs, stomach, spots, scars, feet, hair (whichever part of your body you feel strongly about) I am clumsy, too tall, short.

I choose to

- ❖ Accept myself anyway
- ❖ Let it go
- ❖ Release the feeling
- ❖ Feel good about myself
- ❖ Like my body and imperfections
- ❖ Feel more comfortable with myself
- ❖ Stop worrying about it
- ❖ Accept what I can't change
- ❖ Be healthy

What is the intensity of the feeling now?
Do theGamut

Remember to tap for whatever may come into your mind as this will be connected to the issue. When did it start? Tap for any uncomfortable memories about your body image.

EFT for CONFIDENCE

Create a statement that describes how you feel (or work through all of them, one at a time). Look at the choices below and choose the best match or add your own.

Measure the intensity of the feeling on a scale of 1-10

Even though I lack confidence when: -

I am in lectures, tutorials, in a new relationship, meeting new people, speaking in public, doing a presentation, driving, doing DIY, with new technology, at interviews, cooking, at the gym

I choose to

- ❖ Stay calm and relaxed
- ❖ Release the feeling
- ❖ Believe in myself
- ❖ Trust myself
- ❖ Take one step at a time
- ❖ Overcome my anxiety
- ❖ Not worry about anyone else
- ❖ Be calm and confident
- ❖ Feel in control
- ❖ Be in control

What is the intensity of the feeling now?
Do the Gamut

Tap for any memories or events which are contributing to how you feel. When did you start to feel like this? What was going on your life.

EFT for FEARS

Create a statement that describes how you feel (or work through all of them, one at a time). Look at the choices below and choose the best match or add your own.

Measure the intensity of the feeling on a scale of 1-10

Even though I am scared of: -

Failure, rejection, not being good enough, not being loved, dying, losing (a loved one), change, speaking in public / groups, heights, snakes, creepy crawlies, being in a small space, crowds, pain, flying, needles, injections, doctors and dentists, cats, dogs, mice or birds.

I choose to

- ❖ Release the fear
- ❖ Believe in myself
- ❖ Trust myself
- ❖ Take things in my stride
- ❖ Overcome my fear
- ❖ Concentrate
- ❖ Be calm and confident
- ❖ Feel in control
- ❖ Be in control

What is the intensity of the feeling now?
Do the Gamut

Tap for any memories or events which are contributing to how you feel. When did you start to feel like this? What was going on your life?

EFT for HABITS

Create a statement that describes your habits (work through them, one at a time). Look at the choices below and choose the best match or add your own.

Measure the intensity of the feeling on a scale of 1-10

Start with your most annoying habit.

Even though I can't stop (Whichever it is)

Biting my nails, checking my phone, talking to myself, cracking my knuckles, swearing, feeling sorry for myself, procrastinating, eating rubbish, arguing with everyone, gnashing my teeth, chewing gum, exaggerating, being aggressive …

I choose to

- ❖ Stop
- ❖ Believe in myself
- ❖ Change
- ❖ Trust myself
- ❖ Stay calm and in control
- ❖ Stop worrying
- ❖ Accept myself anyway
- ❖ Release the habit
- ❖ Feel in control

What is the intensity of the feeling now?
Do the Gamut

Tap for any memories that may be connected to these habits – when did they start?

EFT for ADDICTIONS and CRAVINGS

Your choices here are slightly different but again choose the one that is the best match (or choose your own)

Even though I really want / need   (Score 1-10 for the strength of your craving)

A cigarette, a glass of wine, an energy drink, caffeine (coke, tea, coffee) chocolate, sugar (biscuits, cake, ice cream), to spend some money, shoes / clothes, to gamble, fresh bread, a beer, crisps, a MacDonald's (your favourite food), Others?

For these be as specific as you can – if your chocolate craving is for Galaxy or Dairy Milk then say so! Likewise, if your craving is for a Red Bull, then say so!

I choose to

❖ Resist
❖ Do without
❖ Break the pattern
❖ Cut down
❖ Be satisfied with one
❖ Release the craving
❖ Have water instead
❖ Take control

> Do as many rounds as you need to bring the craving down - It may come back!

What is the intensity of the feeling now?
Do the Gamut

Tap for any memories or events which are contributing to how you feel. When did you start to feel like this?

EFT for SMOKING

Create a statement that describes how you feel (or work through all of them, one at a time). Look at the choices below and choose the best match or add your own.

Measure the intensity of the feeling on a scale of 1-10

Even though

I can't imagine not smoking, I need cigarettes to cope, stay calm, relax, socialise, I'm scared I will put on weight if I stop, I won't know what to do with my hands, I need a cigarette after a meal, with a drink, when I am on the phone, driving, I have smoked since I was..., I smoke when I am bored, tense, as a reward, I have tried before, it is too hard to give up, I don't believe I can stop, I am addicted.

I choose to

❖ Believe I can stop
❖ Release the craving
❖ Relax without them
❖ Cut down slowly
❖ Break the link with tea, coffee, beer wine
❖ Break the habit

What is the intensity of the feeling now?
Do the Gamut

Tap for any memories or events linked to smoking which may be contributing to your habit.

KEEP GOING!!

EFT for PANIC

Create a statement that describes how you feel (or work through all of them, one at a time). Look at the choices below and choose the best match or add your own.

Measure the intensity of the feeling on a scale of 1-10

Even though

My heart is racing, I am shaking, I am having palpitations, I am scared I am having a heart attack, I think I am dying, I I expect to be panicky when...., I panic when I think about.....

I choose to

❖ Stay calm and relaxed
❖ Breathe deeply and slowly
❖ Release the feeling
❖ Believe I am healthy
❖ Release my fear of dying
❖ Break the pattern
❖ Feel in control
❖ Slow my heart rate
❖ Heal

What is the intensity of the feeling now?
Do the Gamut

Tap for any memories or events when you had panic attacks which are contributing to how you feel now.

EFT for REJECTION

Create a statement that describes how you feel (or work through all of them, one at a time). Look at the choices below and choose the best match or add your own.

Measure the intensity of the feeling on a scale of 1-10

Even though

I feel rejected, hurt, unwanted, humiliated, lost , cheated, empty, worthless, sick inside, betrayed, angry, I can't stop crying, I can't stop thinking about him/her, I can't face anyone, I don't deserve this, it's so unfair.

I choose to

- ❖ Heal the hurt
- ❖ Accept it's over
- ❖ Forgive him / her
- ❖ Move on with my life
- ❖ Learn from this experience
- ❖ Stop grieving
- ❖ Release the physical pain
- ❖ Stay calm
- ❖ Release my anger
- ❖ Take care of myself

What is the intensity of the feeling now?
Do the Gamut

Tap for any memories or events which are contributing to how you feel. When did you start to feel like this?

EFT for BULLYING and HARASSMENT

Create a statement that describes how you feel (or work through all of them, one at a time). Look at the choices below and choose the best match or add your own.

Measure the intensity of the feeling on a scale of 1-10

Even though

I am being bullied/ harassed, I am scared of bullies, I feel intimidated, they say horrible things, they make my life hell, I don't stand up to them, I let them get away with it, I can't escape them, no-one believes me about the bullying/harassment, I am being tormented

I choose to

❖ Ignore what they say
❖ Get advice
❖ Report them
❖ Be more resilient
❖ Ensure I am not alone with them
❖ Tell them that they are not succeeding
❖ Move on with my life
❖ Take care of myself
❖ Stay calm
❖ Keep a record

Have you got a copy of the Bullying Policy?

What is the intensity of the feeling now?
Do the Gamut

Tap for any memories or events which are contributing to how you feel. When did you start to feel like this?

EFT for MILD DEPRESSION

Create a statement that describes how you feel (or work through all of them, one at a time). Look at the choices below and choose the best match or add your own.

Measure the intensity of the feeling on a scale of 1-10

Even though

I feel low, sad, bad, miserable, lost, unwanted, worthless, desperate, hopeless, powerless, drained, exhausted, suicidal.

I choose to

- ❖ Heal the emotional pain
- ❖ Move on with my life
- ❖ Learn from this experience
- ❖ Take care of myself
- ❖ Believe things will improve
- ❖ Look forward
- ❖ Feel more positive
- ❖ Do some exercise
- ❖ Stop dwelling on things

What is the intensity of the feeling now?
Do the Gamut

Tap for any memories or events which are contributing to how you feel. When did you start to feel like this? What was going on your life?

EFT for MOTIVATION

Create a statement that describes how you feel (or work through all of them, one at a time). Look at the choices below and choose the best match or add your own.

Measure the intensity of the feeling on a scale of 1-10

Even though

I can't be bothered with anything, I feel fed up, lethargic, nothing interests me, I don't want to do anything, I have no energy.

I choose to

- ❖ Feel energised
- ❖ Find something that I would like to do most
- ❖ Stop procrastinating
- ❖ Start one thing at a time
- ❖ Not to feel overwhelmed by everything I need do
- ❖ Commit to a task with a friend then be accountable
- ❖ Avoid distractions
- ❖ Spend time with positive people
- ❖ Read and absorb motivation quotations

What is the intensity of the feeling now?
Do the Gamut

Tap for any memories or events which are contributing to how you feel. When did you start to feel like this? What was going on your life?

EFT for ASSERTION

Create a statement that describes how you feel (or work through all of them, one at a time). Look at the choices below and choose the best match or add your own.

Measure the intensity of the feeling on a scale of 1-10

Even though

I am a bit of a wimp, I feel intimidated, manipulated, overwhelmed, pressured, inferior, vulnerable, I can't say no, I can't express my feelings, I don't stand up for myself, I hate criticism, I crumble when someone shouts at me, I feel powerless.

I choose to

- ❖ Say what I mean
- ❖ Be unafraid
- ❖ Trust my judgement
- ❖ Be true to my beliefs and values
- ❖ Be calm in my responses
- ❖ Say no without feeling guilty
- ❖ Stick to my principles
- ❖ Ignore confrontation

What is the intensity of the feeling now?
Do the Gamut

Tap for any memories or events when you felt intimidated which are contributing to how you feel now.

EFT for PERFECTIONISM

Create a statement that describes how you feel (or work through all of them, one at a time). Look at the choices below and choose the best match or add your own.

Measure the intensity of the feeling on a scale of 1-10

Even though

I need to be perfect, I will never be good enough, I feel like an imposter, nothing is good enough, I am a failure, I need to work harder, I will never be contented unless….,I need to achieve more….

I choose to

- ❖ Believe I am doing my best
- ❖ Trust in my ability
- ❖ Acknowledge my achievements
- ❖ Accept that no one is perfect
- ❖ Learn from my mistakes and move on
- ❖ Stop driving myself so hard
- ❖ Feel good about myself
- ❖ Release my negative beliefs

What is the intensity of the feeling now?
Do the Gamut

Tap for any memories or events which are contributing to how you feel. When did you start to feel like this?

EFT for WORKLOAD

Create a statement that describes how you feel (or work through all of them, one at a time). Look at the choices below and choose the best match or add your own.

Measure the intensity of the feeling on a scale of 1-10

Even though

I am out of my depth, I can't cope, I feel overwhelmed, I am under too much pressure, I have too much to do, too much is expected, I have no time to myself, I am working all hours

I choose to

- ❖ Plan effectively
- ❖ Prioritise
- ❖ Be realistic
- ❖ Be assertive and say something
- ❖ Release the overwhelm
- ❖ Believe in my ability to achieve
- ❖ Release the pressure
- ❖ Stay calm and in control
- ❖ Maintain a work life balance

What is the intensity of the feeling now?
Do the Gamut

Tap for any memories or events when you had these feelings which are contributing to how you feel now.

Don't be afraid to ask for help!

EFT for EXAM STRESS

Create a statement that describes how you feel (or work through all of them, one at a time). Look at the choices below and choose the best match or add your own.

Measure the intensity of the feeling on a scale of 1-10

Even though

I am scared of failing, I can't concentrate, I am not absorbing anything, I feel numb, I don't understand it, I can't cope, I feel overwhelmed, I am expected to do well, I am exhausted

I choose to

- ❖ Plan effectively
- ❖ Start early without procrastinating
- ❖ Prioritise and pace myself
- ❖ Absorb and remember
- ❖ Not let myself down
- ❖ Release the overwhelm
- ❖ Believe in my ability to achieve
- ❖ Stay calm and in control
- ❖ Get regular sleep

What is the intensity of the feeling now?
Do the Gamut

Tap for any memories or events when you had these feelings which are contributing to how you feel now.

Don't be afraid to ask for help for anything you don't understand!

EFT for PRESENTATIONS and SPEAKING

Create a statement that describes how you feel (or work through all of them, one at a time). Look at the choices below and choose the best match or add your own.

Measure the intensity of the feeling on a scale of 1-10

Even though

I feel conspicuous, nervous, worried about what people will think, I am scared, I will forget my words, no one will listen, I am afraid, I will make a mistake, everyone will see how shaky I am.

I choose to

- ❖ Stay calm and relaxed
- ❖ Practice, practice, practice
- ❖ Breathe deeply and slowly before starting
- ❖ Do my best
- ❖ Focus on my delivery
- ❖ Speak clearly
- ❖ Do my best
- ❖ Accept that the audience are unlikely to know what I have missed out!

What is the intensity of the feeling now?
Do the Gamut

Tap for any memories or events when you had these feelings which are contributing to how you feel now.

(Often these feelings go back to school when you possibly made a mistake in front of the class and they laughed)

EFT for INTERVIEW NERVES

Create a statement that describes how you feel (or work through all of them, one at a time). Look at the choices below and choose the best match or add your own.

Measure the intensity of the feeling on a scale of 1-10

Even though

I am scared of: failing, making a fool of myself, being tongue tied, I won't be able to answer the questions, I will let myself down, I won't ask the right questions at the end, I will get brain freeze. I won't make the right impression.

I choose to

- ❖ Remember to breathe deeply and evenly
- ❖ Think carefully before I answer questions
- ❖ Speak slowly and clearly
- ❖ provide as much information as I can
- ❖ Remember what I want to say
- ❖ Do my best
- ❖ Stay calm
- ❖ Concentrate
- ❖ Stop worrying
- ❖ Think clearly

What is the intensity of the feeling now?
Do the Gamut

Tap for any memories connected to previous interviews which are contributing to how you feel.

EFT for DYSLEXIA

Create a statement that describes how you feel (or work through all of them, one at a time). Look at the choices below and choose the best match or add your own.

Measure the intensity of the feeling on a scale of 1-10

Even though

I am hopeless at reading, I can't spell, I get really tense trying to read aloud, I get muddled up, the words don't make sense, my writing is awful, I get confused, I panic, I have no confidence, I avoid reading and writing. Others?

I choose to

- ❖ Accept myself anyway
- ❖ Break this pattern
- ❖ Believe I can change
- ❖ See and understand clearly
- ❖ Feel calm and in control
- ❖ Unscramble things in my mind
- ❖ Spell (the word) correctly

What is the intensity of the feeling now?
Do the Gamut

Tap for any memories or events when you had these feelings which are contributing to how you feel now.

EFT for ADHD

Attention Deficit Hyperactivity Disorder

Create a statement that describes how you feel (or work through all of them, one at a time). Look at the choices below and choose the best match or add your own.

Measure the intensity of the feeling on a scale of 1-10

Even though

I am hyper right now, I am talking too fast, I can't sit still, I can't concentrate, I don't want to listen, I want to do something else, I feel frustrated, different, confused, angry, hopeless, I can't control myself, I believe I must be stupid, I can't take anything in. Others?

I choose to

- ❖ Accept myself anyway
- ❖ Stay calm and listen
- ❖ Release the tension
- ❖ Believe I can change
- ❖ Sit still
- ❖ Break the pattern
- ❖ Feel in control

What is the intensity of the feeling now?
Do the Gamut

Tap for any memories or events when you had these feelings which are contributing to how you feel now.

EFT for OCD

Obsessive Compulsive Disorder

Create a statement that describes how you feel (or work through all of them, one at a time). Look at the choices below and choose the best match or add your own.

Measure the intensity of the feeling on a scale of 1-10

Even though

I need to check....., I want to check....., I can't stop.....,I get anxious when....., I am scared I will....., unless I do....

(Whatever the compulsion is)

I choose to

- ❖ Stop
- ❖ Release the need / habit
- ❖ Believe I can change
- ❖ Take my time
- ❖ Break the pattern
- ❖ Feel in control
- ❖ Accept that I am not perfect
- ❖ Stay calm
- ❖ Do things differently

What is the intensity of the feeling now?
Do the Gamut

Tap for any memories or events when you had this compulsion which are contributing to how you feel now.

EFT for SLEEP

Create a statement that describes how you feel (or work through all of them, one at a time). Look at the choices below and choose the best match or add your own.

Measure the intensity of the feeling on a scale of 1-10

Tap before you try to sleep

Even though

I am worried that I might not sleep, I can't stop thinking about ....., my mind is racing, I am too wound up to sleep, I am wide awake, I am overtired, I expect to wake in the night

I choose to

- ❖ Relax and let go
- ❖ Switch off
- ❖ Sleep through the night
- ❖ Sleep soundly
- ❖ Break the pattern
- ❖ Relax my body
- ❖ Sleep until 7.00 (whatever time you wish to wake)

What is the intensity of the feeling now?
Do the Gamut

Tap for any memories or events when you had sleep problems which are contributing to how you feel now.

Please *note that smoking may take a bit longer than some of the other things, but it can be done. Use the same process for wine, beer, spirits, crisps, chocolate, biscuits or any other food or drink craving.*

When the intensity or strength of an emotion is over 5 then it feels as if the emotion is in control. When it is below 5 then you feel in control of the emotion. It feels more manageable and matters less. The lower the score, the better you will feel.

After following the above procedure, if the emotion is still bothersome but has come down a little then say "Even though I *still* have this fear, craving, anxiety about....." I choose to let it go.

As you tap – say "This remaining fear, craving anxiety about..." and proceed as before.

BLOCKAGES and SELF SABOTAGE
Whatever you are tapping for, think when it first started.

WHat was going on?

WHere were you?

WHeN was it?

WHo were you with?

HoW did the situation develop?

WHy does it upset you?

Tap for the memory and why it upset you – deal with all the aspects of the situation. Some may be deep rooted but when you think of a plant, it's those with the deepest and strongest roots that grow more.

If you know there is something holding you back but have no idea what it is, have a look at old photos and see if they trigger anything for you.

You can also say
"Even though I don't know what the problem is"
"Even though I don't know how I feel "
"I choose to let it go"
"I accept myself anyway"

Remember that the subconscious is aware and may have blocked a memory in order to protect you, and the conscious mind may not have a clue!

CONCLUSION

Life during a pandemic is tough for all of us, regardless of personal circumstances. We all experience stress and anxiety due to a mixture of uncertainty, fear, loss, redundancy, illness, lack of income, loneliness, and frustration. Maybe the end is in sight with the discovery of the vaccine, but I am sure that stress levels amongst students is here to stay. As I said in the beginning, stress is something that we are all familiar with but perhaps you did not realise quite how it can affect every aspect of our lives. I hope this book has offered some enlightenment and you are now able to recognise, understand and act when you are struggling to cope.

Ruth Fogg - January 2021

STRESSWORX

Positive Solutions for Peace of Mind

RUTH FOGG
Therapist - Educator - Speaker - Author

Ruth specialises in providing practical skills and solutions to understand and manage stress in both personal and professional situations.

As a **THERAPIST** - She offers individual therapy to adults, teenagers and children to explore and address the wide range of issues that result in stress, including negative behaviour patterns, habits, fears, phobias, cravings and addictions, low self-esteem, lack of confidence, exam nerves, panic attacks – anything that holds people back at home or work.

As an **EDUCATOR** - Ruth offers workshops in the workplace, school college or university which include compliance with the law, stress audits and practical solutions to understand, manage and control stress

As a **SPEAKER** – Ruth speaks about stress "The Invisible Enemy" "Happy People – Happy Places " "Too Much Monkey Business" "Is Stress Self Inflicted? " "Ephebiphobia". And of course, "Tackling Tough Times"

As an **AUTHOR** – Ruth has written "Stress Tips for Busy People", "Tapping for Teens" "Stress n' Stuff - Tackling Teenage Mental Health" and "Stress n' Stuff – Tackling Tough Times. She intends to continue the Stress N' Stuff series.

Her qualifications include a Diploma and MSc in Counselling Psychology, Teaching, Coaching, Reiki, Hypnosis, Emotional Freedom Technique and Stress Management. She has been in business since 2002.

Ruth has a background in teaching and youth work. She was Head of the Youth Service in the London Borough of Ealing for twelve years and is an Honorary Fellow of Brunel University. She was the chairperson of the Centre for Youth Work Studies at Brunel for ten years. As a freelance trainer and qualified Assessor, she has delivered qualifications in youth work for throughout London and the South east.

As an Ofsted Inspector she has undertaken inspections and numerous pre – inspection checks for youth services all over the country. Until recently she was a Director of YMCA London South West and Middlesex Young Peoples Clubs. She was also a Trustee for MIND in Ealing and YMCA Training.

After taking early retirement in 2002, she developed her stress consultancy but continued youth work training and assessment.

Ruth is a member of the General Hypnotherapy Standards Council; Spelthorne Business Forum; The Complementary and Natural Healthcare Council and the Professional Speakers Association. She is a Stress Advisor and Fellow of The International Stress Management Association.

She is married with two adult sons and lives in Wraysbury, near Windsor where she is an Associate Governor at the primary school and a founder member of "wraysbury matters", promoting wellbeing in the community.

TESTIMONIALS

"Not only is Ruth an expert in Stress Management she is a excellent presenter. She has a wonderful way of putting her subject across, keeping it simple, using humour and totally engaging her audience. I have heard her speak on a number of occasions and am always keen to listen, learn & enjoy again"
Mike Wylie – Director Midas Plus

"Ruth, is an exceptional business coach, consultant, and trainer. Ruth has a lovely disposition that immediately put you at ease. Her experience and expertise is very evident, Ruth is high qualified and competent and has an ability to add value to any organisation that she works with."
Dr Carlton Brown PhD, MBA PGDiP F.APS

Ruth is a Stress Management professional who presents sound advice, tools & techniques in her field. Having experienced a consultation with Ruth, I can recommend success in the service she delivers and wouldn't hesitate in making recommendation to others where I see they would benefit.
Mandy Robson – Head of Health and Safety at British Print Industries Federation

"I have known Ruth for many years and therefore always aware of her commitment to helping young and old with any mental health related needs. But perhaps it was seeing Ruth presenting at group events or being interviewed on the radio that my admiration grew. This was not only for her wide knowledge in the field of mental health, but for her absolute ability to empathise and honestly believe that there can be solutions. In a world where it can be so easy to give up, or be abandoned by others, I am comforted that Ruth and her life-changing books can be called upon." -
Lynn Holden Director and Founder of Swan Radio

Ruth is not only a great listener she has fantastic practical ways of helping. I discovered this at a particularly

challenging time of my life when I was suffering from reactive anxiety and depression. Coping Skills once learned are useful for all the difficult times.
Senior NHS Manager

Thank you Ruth for helping out our colleague, he was having a particularly difficult time emotionally, very stressed, and with your help and therapy he has returned to work with a sense of purpose, a clear mind – a fresh start.

In all the years I have known him he has never been this confident and in control, thank you, it was difficult for him through lockdown, he was off work unwell with a chest infection, but controlled his anxiety with 'tapping' and its really helped.
Debbie Keen. Director HDS FREIGHT Ltd

If you suffer from stress, visit Ruth. I have personally benefited from her coaching, the session included EFT and the result was miraculous, EFT is a quick process to release trapped energy, the same as bursting an emotional energy balloon, it helped me let go of grief. She presented to the young people at the charity that I work for and they were queuing up to ask her advice at the end of the session.
Rose Evans, Community Voice Manager at Nacro

Printed in Great Britain
by Amazon